LAB MANUAL

TO ACCOMPANY THE COMPLETE GUIDE TO NETWORKING AND NETWORK+

Michael W. Graves

THOMSON

DELMAR LEARNING

Australia • Canada • Mexico • Singapore • Spain • United Kingdom • United States

THOMSON

DELMAR LEARNING

Lab Manual to accompany The Complete Guide to Networking and Network+, 2e
by Michael W. Graves

Vice President, Technology and Trades SBU:
Alar Elken

Editorial Director:
Sandy Clark

Senior Acquisitions Editor:
Stephen Helba

Senior Development Editor:
Michelle Ruelos Cannistraci

Marketing Director:
Dave Gaza

Senior Channel Manager:
Dennis Williams

Marketing Coordinator:
Stacey Wiktorek

Production Director:
Mary Ellen Black

Production Manager:
Andrew Crouth

Production Coordinator:
Dawn Jacobson

Art/Design Coordinator:
Francis Hogan

Senior Editorial Assistant:
Dawn Daugherty

Library of Congress Cataloging-in-Publication Data:

Library of Congress Control Number: 2005926879

Lab Manual to accompany Guide to Networking and Network+, 2e / Michael W. Graves

ISBN: 1418019453

NOTICE TO THE READER

Publisher does not warrant or guarantee any of the products described herein or perform any independent analysis in connection with any of the product information contained herein. Publisher does not assume, and expressly disclaims, any obligation to obtain and include information other than that provided to it by the manufacturer.

The reader is expressly warned to consider and adopt all safety precautions that might be indicated by the activities herein and to avoid all potential hazards. By following the instructions contained herein, the reader willingly assumes all risks in connection with such instructions.

The publisher makes no representation or warranties of any kind, including but not limited to, the warranties of fitness for particular purpose or merchantability, nor are any such representations implied with respect to the material set forth herein, and the publisher takes no responsibility with respect to such material. The publisher shall not be liable for any special, consequential, or exemplary damages resulting, in whole or part, from the readers' use of, or reliance upon, this material.

TABLE OF CONTENTS

WELCOME TO THE NETWORKING AND NETWORK+ LAB MANUAL

Greetings, and welcome to the world of Network+. This book is designed to accompany the book, *The Complete Guide to Networking and Network+, 2e,* and contains several hands-on exercises designed to supplement the text. However, it can also be used as a stand-alone manual. This lab manual accompanies the text, but it is not designed to follow the text chapter by chapter. Where appropriate, I make references to relevant material in the text. In order to perform the following labs, you will need to have a certain amount of equipment. Ideally, the classroom should be equipped with RJ-45 wall jacks. The cable from these jacks should run through the walls to a corner of the classroom with easy access for more than one person at a time. The cable should drop from the ceiling to a patch panel. Near the patch panel should be a small shelf or rack for the classroom hub.

Each student should have a computer that can have its OS removed and reinstalled. You will also need a dedicated server available to the classroom. This can be the instructor's machine, if necessary. In addition, the labs will require a short list of supplemental equipment and software.

MATERIALS THAT WILL BE REQUIRED TO COMPLETE ALL LABS

In order to assure that the classrooms are fully equipped for all the labs in this book, I have prepared a complete list of all materials that will be required. These items are as follows:

- Enough copies of Windows 2000 Server or Advanced Server for each student

- Enough copies of Windows 2000 Professional for each student

- A student machine for each student (see next section for basic requirements)

- A NIC, with drivers, for each machine (should not yet be installed)

- Dedicated classroom server (can be the instructor's machine if necessary) with a tape drive installed

- Tape appropriate for the drive

- A hub or switch

- 18- or 24-port patch panel

- Punch down tool appropriate for the patch panel to be used in the lab (recommend one for each student)

- Network cable crimping tool (recommend one for each student)

- Bulk CAT5 or CAT5e twisted-pair cable

- CAT5 terminators (sufficient quantity for each student to make a patch cable and a crossover cable, with spares for errors)

- RJ-45 terminators

- Ten high-density floppy diskettes for each student

- A DOS or Windows boot diskette

- Technician's tool kits (recommend one for each student)

- A roll of adding machine tape

- A box of #10 envelopes

CLASSROOM MACHINES

In this particular series of labs, the instructor machine and the student machines will have to be able to run the same OS and services. Therefore, they can all be identical. As I indicated in the list above, the NICs in the student workstations should not yet be installed. Students will be installing these cards themselves in one of the earlier labs. Here are the minimum recommended specifications:

- Pentium II 500Mhz

- 128MB RAM minimum (recommend 256MB)

- 6.4GB hard disk drive

- VGA graphics

- 24X CD-ROM

- 3.5" 1.44MB floppy diskette drive

- Pointing device (mouse or trackball)

- Keyboard

- VGA monitor

In addition, it would be useful to have a CD-RW drive installed at least on the instructor's workstation.

SUPPLEMENTAL MATERIALS

In addition to the jacks and cabling I mentioned earlier, the classroom should be equipped with the following items:

- Overhead VGA projector

- 10/100 switch or hub

- Advanced cable tester

- Internet access

- One computer with Windows 98 installed

There are several items that will not be actively used in the labs but that would be good to have around for "show and tell." Among these are:

- Coaxial patch cables

- T-connectors

- Coaxial terminators

- A vampire clamp

- A length of fiber-optics cable

- Fiber-optics terminators

- A CSU/DSU

LAB ADDRESSING AND NAMING SCHEMES

It is not necessary to plan out an addressing scheme in advance, since you will be doing that in one of the labs. However, for consistency, a naming convention is in order. For the purposes of these labs, the Instructor Machine will be SERVERMAIN. Student computers will be named STUDENT1, STUDENT2, STUDENT3, and so on until all systems are named. At any given point these machines may be acting as servers or workstations.

In Lab Four, you will set up a classroom peer-to-peer network. During this session, you will apply static IP addresses to each machine and will assign addresses at that time. In Lab Five, you will be configuring the student computers to dual boot between Windows 2000 Professional and Windows 2000 Server. The instructor machine will act as the DHCP server and assign addresses dynamically, except for a lab on DHCP, where the students will take turns being the active server.

CONFIGURING THE INSTRUCTOR MACHINE

The instructor's machine should be configured from the start to be running Windows 2000 Server or Advanced Server. The following procedures should be followed if you need to install Windows 2000 Server:

INSTALLING WINDOWS 2000 SERVER

If the computer is configured to boot from the CD, boot to the Windows 2000 (W2K) Server installation CD, and type CD I386. If the machine will not boot from the CD, then insert the W2K Server CD into a working machine and browse to the BOOTDISK directory. Have four blank, formatted high-density floppy diskettes ready and run the MAKEBT32 program. This program will lead you through the process of making the installation diskettes.

Since most computers will successfully boot from a CD-ROM, the following instructions are based on this method. The differences between this method and a diskette-based method are minimal and exist only in the text-based

portion of the process. (That, by the way, is the part of installation that takes place before the computer reboots into a graphical user interface with full point-and-click capability.)

1. Make sure your computer is configured to boot from CD. Place the installation CD-ROM in the drive and reboot the computer. Setup will start and begin by copying a minimum file set to memory on your computer. You will be prompted to press <F6> if there are any third-party drivers you need, such as a SCSI adapter that Setup cannot recognize. You will need these drivers available on floppy diskette. It is very likely that you may have to make use of another computer to create these diskettes from the CD-ROM that shipped with the device. Each manufacturer has its own way of making these diskettes, so look for instructions in the manual (if it shipped with one), or check the CD-ROM for a read-me file that explains the process. When Setup reaches the point of requiring those files, it will prompt you to insert that diskette.

2. When the files have been copied, you will be presented with a screen with the following options:

   - Run Windows 2000 Setup. Press <Enter> for this option.

   - Repair an existing Windows 2000 installation. Press <R> for this option.

   - Exit without installing Windows 2000. Press <F3> for this option.

3. Press Enter to run Windows 2000 Setup. Here, you will be warned you could possibly lose data if you continue. The options are:

   - Continue Setup. Press <C> for this option.

   - Quit Setup. Press <F3> for this option.

4. Press <C> to continue. You are now presented with the licensing agreement. Press <Page Down> in order to read the agreement. Press <F8> to accept the terms or <Esc> to reject them. If you press <Esc>, the installation will be aborted.

5. After you press <F8>, you are presented with a screen that shows all available fixed disks and all partitions on each disk. If the computer on which you have chosen to install Windows 2000 Server has preexisting operating systems and/or data, these should all be deleted. Highlight each partition in turn, pressing <D> to delete the partition. There will be some additional instructions to confirm that you wish to delete these partitions. In each step, confirm that you wish to delete the partition. Now on Drive C, press <C> to create a new partition. Do **not** select the option of using all available space. Use approximately fifty percent of drive C for your boot partition and leave the remaining space available as Free Space. Once that is completed, highlight your newly created partition and press <Enter>.

6. Now you will be prompted to select whether you want to format the partition using FAT or NTFS. Select NTFS and continue.

7. Next will appear a screen showing the progress as your partition is formatted. Depending on the size of your drive, this could take anywhere from a few minutes to the rest of your natural life.

8. Next, Setup will initialize and begin to copy files to the newly formatted partition. There is approximately 325MB of data to be copied, so this will take a while. When this is completed, you will be prompted to remove any disks from your computer and notified that the system will reboot in fifteen seconds. Pressing <Enter> will restart it immediately.

9. On this reboot, you will enter the graphical phase of Setup, and the Setup Wizard will begin. You now have mouse support. Replace the installation CD. You'll need it for the subsequent steps. Click Next to continue the installation.

10. You will go into a hardware detection phase. This can take a while, and your screen may do some funny things while it's happening. This is nothing to worry about. Let it proceed.

11. Next, you are prompted to enter your Regional Settings. When you're finished, click Next. You will be prompted to enter your name and organization. The name is mandatory, whereas the organization is optional.

12. Here is where you enter the twenty-five-digit product key for your Windows 2000 Server. This is found on a sticker affixed to the jewel case that housed the CD.

13. Now you will be asked to enter the number of licenses. You have the option of Per Server or Per Seat. Select Per Server and type in 500 for the number of licenses. (The legalities of licensing issues will be discussed in Lab Five.)

14. Next comes the screen into which you enter the computer name and administrator password. For the computer name, enter SERVERMAIN. For the purpose of this classroom(áetup, use password as the password for this computer and all student machines. You will need to enter the password a second time in order to confirm it, and if you accidentally mistype it, you will have to type it over both times.

15. Now you are prompted to install any optional components you desire. Skip this step. You will install components as you need them.

16. The next step is to set your time, date, and time zone. If your CMOS is correctly configured, time and date should already be accurate, but the time zone defaults to Pacific Standard. Microsoft assumes everybody lives in Seattle.

17. You will now enter the portion of setup that installs networking components. By default, Client for Microsoft Networks, File and Printer Sharing, and TCP/IP are installed. TCP/IP, unless told otherwise, will assume a DHCP server already exists on the network. You will be given the option of statically configuring an IP address and installing other components. Statically configure the machine to 192.168.0.110 and install NWLink IPX/SPX/NetBIOS Compatible Transport Protocol.

18. The next screen will prompt you to either join a workgroup or an existing domain. Select Workgroup and leave the default Workgroup as is. Click Next.

19. Setup will now copy several files to your hard drive and initialize your registry settings. Temporary files will be deleted and your system will restart.

20. Next, you need to promote your computer to the status of Domain Controller. To do this, Click Start, Run... and type into the command field dcpromo. You will get a screen like the one in **Figure I.1**. Click Next.

21. The screen that pops up next is the Domain Controller Type screen. Your options are "Domain controller for a new domain" and "Additional domain controller for an existing domain." Select Domain controller for a new domain and click next.

22. Now you will be asked if you wish to create a new domain tree or if you wish to create a new child domain. Create a new domain tree. Now you are asked if you want to create a new forest of

Figure I.1 Opening the Active Directory Wizard

domain trees or if you wish to place this new domain into an existing forest. Create a new domain forest.

23. Now you will be asked to name your domain. For the purposes of these lab exercises, type `classroom.com` into the field and click next. On the next screen, where you are prompted for a NetBIOS Domain Name accept the default and click Next. Also accept the defaults and click Next for the following two screens—Database and Log Locations and Shared System Volume.

24. Since this is the first controller on your domain, the next screen will be a warning that it could not find a DNS controller. Don't worry about that screen. Simply click OK and the next screen will lead you through configuring DNS on this machine.

25. On the Configure DNS screen that follows, click Yes, install and configure DNS on this server (recommended). On the Permissions screen that appears, the default is Permissions compatible with pre-Windows 2000 server. Leave the default as is and click Next. You will now be prompted to enter a

Directory Services Restore Mode Administrator Password. Type in `password` once again and continue.

26. The Configuring Active Directory dialog box will now appear. This process can take quite some time, so be patient and do not attempt to restart the machine or shut it down during this process. When it is finished, restart the computer. Your server is ready to go.

Preparing the Student Machines

The students will install operating systems during the lab sessions. Therefore, the only preparation that is required is to make sure that the hard disk drives are completely wiped clean. The easiest way to do this is to use a Windows 98 Startup diskette to start the machines and from the A: prompt, type `fdisk`.

Select Option 4, Display Partition Information, to see how many partitions are configured on the machine. They should all be deleted. Next select Option 3, Delete Partition or Logical DOS Drive and delete all partitions on the drive. Do not create any new partitions, as this will be done in a later lab.

NETWORK WIRING

INTRODUCTION

One of the more common tasks that befalls a network engineer is that of preparing cabling and/or wiring patch panels. Neither one of these tasks requires much in the way of mental stress, but they do call on your physical dexterity a bit.

By the time you are finished, you will have prepared the patch cable that you will use to connect your computer to the network. You will also have made a crossover cable that you can add to your tool kit, and you will have learned how to wire a patch panel in a wiring or server closet. So do whatever warm-ups you choose for fine-tuning your coordination and let's go.

MATERIALS

For these exercises, you're going to need the following items:

- Network cable crimping tool
- Bulk CAT5 or CAT5e twisted-pair cable
- RJ-45 terminators
- 18- or 24-port patch panel
- Punch down tool

NETWORK+ EXAM OBJECTIVES COVERED IN THIS LAB

1.4 Recognize media connectors and describe their uses.

1.5 Recognize media types and describe their uses.

3.3 Identify the appropriate tool for a given wiring task (For example: wire crimper, media tester/certifier, punch down tool or tone generator).

EXERCISE 1: SHOW AND TELL

The instructor should collect as many of the following items as possible and pass them around the room, explaining their function and how they are used.

- Length of coaxial cable
- BNC connector
- T-connector for coaxial cable
- Vampire clamp

- Crimping tool
- Length of twisted-pair cable
- RJ-45 jack
- Wall jack
- Patch panel
- Hub or switch

EXERCISE 2: A TOUR OF THE CRIMPING TOOL

Pick up your crimping tool and examine it. You'll notice three key functions to this tool. **Figure 1.1** will help you find these features if you're new to this tool.

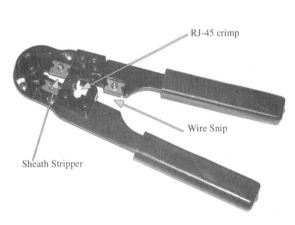

Figure 1.1 The RJ-45 crimping tool

There is a wire-cutting blade, which is used for cutting the lengths of cable. You'll notice that the second set of blades, closer to the end, does not close all the way. These blades are for stripping the outside layer of insulation from the cable. Be careful using this feature. With many of these tools, it is very easy to snip off one or more of the wires inside. You don't want that. Last is the crimping jaw itself. Conveniently

shaped like an RJ-45 jack, it enables you to simply bring the handles together, insert the terminator, and squeeze.

EXERCISE 3: MAKING A PATCH CABLE

Students will need a length of CAT5 or CAT5e twisted-pair cable of the appropriate length to connect their systems to the wall jacks in your room. You'll need an appropriate length of CAT5 or CAT5e cable, two RJ-45 (RJ-45 stands for *registered jack 45)* terminators for the patch cable (but it would probably be a good idea to have extras lying around, just in case), and your crimping tool. This will go much faster if everyone has his or her own crimping tool.

1. Strip approximately 3/4 of an inch to an inch of the outer insulation from each end of the cabling, exposing the four pairs of wire. Do **not** attempt to strip each individual wire.

   NOTE: Most crimping tools have a spacer on the sheath stripper that trims off the correct length for a standard RJ-45 connector. Personally, I find it easier to strip an inch or more. It makes it easier to arrange the wires into the correct order. Once the wires are arranged, flatten them between your fingers and use the wire snips to trim them evenly to the desired length.

2. Note that the wires are arranged in pairs of wires twisted together (hence the name twisted pair). These pairs are green-white/green, brown-white/brown, orange-white/orange, and blue-white/blue. Untwist the pairs and arrange them into the following order: white/orange, orange, white/green, blue, white/blue, green, white/brown, and brown (as shown in **Figure 1.2**).

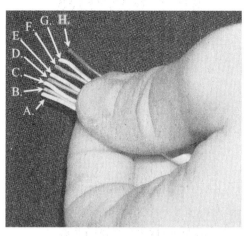

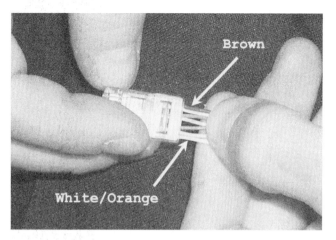

A. White/Orange E. White/Blue
B. Orange F. Green
C. White/Green G. White/Brown
D. Blue H. Brown

Figure 1.2 If you make your strands of wire long enough, they'll be easier to work with.

Figure 1.3 Make sure the ends of the wire go all the way to the tip of the connector.

Figure 1.4 Crimping the connector

3. Making sure the wires stay in the correct order, press them snugly into the connector. With the locking clip facing away from you, the orange pair should be on the left (see **Figure 1.3**).

4. Place the connector into the jaws of the RJ-45 crimp and squeeze the handle firmly together as in **Figure 1.4**.

5. Repeat the process on the other side of your cable and you have a finished patch cable.

EXERCISE 3 DISCUSSION

1. What would be the result of getting two wires crossed when seating them into the connector?

2. List the order of wires as they go into the connector.

3. What does RJ signify?

EXERCISE 4: MAKING A CROSSOVER CABLE

A crossover cable is a handy accessory to have in your gadget bag. It allows you to directly connect two PCs, a notebook to a PC, or any other two devices that normally make use of straight through RJ-45 interfaces. To make one, repeat the above procedures with this exception.

1. One end of the cable will be wired as explained in Exercise 3.

2. The other end will be wired in the following order: White/green, green, white/orange, blue, white/blue, orange, white/brown, brown.

EXERCISE 5: WIRING A PATCH PANEL

Most networks these days bring the cable drops together into a single location and connect them to a patch panel. The patch panel is then labeled

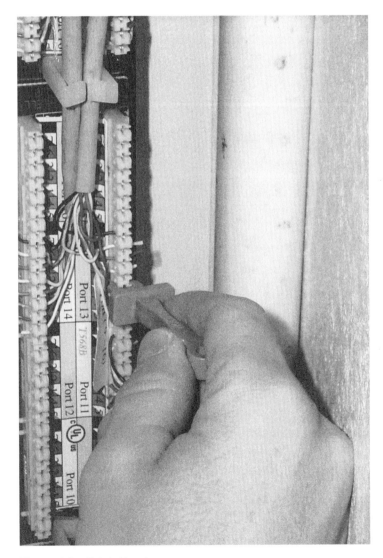

Figure 1.5 Patch Panel

as to what device is attached to what port. That way it is easier to disconnect a specific device from the network or to patch it into a different subnet if necessary. To wire a patch panel, you need the patch panel itself, cable drops, and a punch down tool.

Punch down tools run the gamut from a simple plastic tool to fancy electrical devices that pound the wire into the panel with enough force to knock out an elephant. You can get one from a vendor for around fifteen bucks, or you can use the little plastic one packaged with the wall jacks you buy. It's your preference.

Patch panels generally ship with colored guides to indicate the proper wiring pattern. Note that there are two different standards. The Electronics Industry Association teamed up with the Telecommunications Industry Association to form the EIA/TIA 568A and 568B standards. Make sure you use 568B.

1. Pull down the cable drop you want to wire, run it through the cable channels in the panel, and clip it off to the length you need.

2. Strip off about two inches of the insulation sheath and separate the wire pairs.

3. Trim each individual wire to the correct length to fit the appropriate slot in the back of the patch panel.

4. Line the wire up to the correct slot and press it down firmly with the punch down tool. Repeat the process until all eight wires are seated.

EXERCISE 5 DISCUSSION

1. What makes a patch panel such a convenient device to add to any network?

2. Why wouldn't you want to wire your patch panel to EIA/TIA 568A standards?

INSTALLING AN OS

INTRODUCTION

There are those who argue that installing an operating system (OS) is not a function of a network administrator. Those are the people who either have the luxury of extremely large and diverse staffs, or simply haven't spent enough time in the real world. There will come a time when you will have to install an OS on a new system or completely rebuild an existing one.

MATERIALS

In the following exercises, you will be installing Windows 2000 Professional. In order to complete the exercises you will need to make use of the following items:

- Student machine for each student

- Five high-density floppy diskettes for each student

- One machine configured with Windows 98 (or a DOS or Windows boot diskette)

NETWORK+ EXAM OBJECTIVES COVERED IN THIS LAB

3.2 Identify the basic capabilities needed for client workstations to connect to and use network resources (For example: media, network protocols and peer and server services).

4.6 Given a scenario, determine the impact of modifying, adding or removing network services (For example: DHCP (Dynamic Host Configuration Protocol), DNS (Domain Name Service) and WINS (Windows Internet Name Service)) for network resources and users.

EXERCISE 1: PREPARING A BOOT DISKETTE

Most modern machines will easily boot from the CD-ROM drive, and since the Windows 2000 CD is a bootable CD, you would simply put the CD in the drive, boot the machine, and follow the yellow brick road. For the purpose of these labs, I'm going to give you a worst-case scenario. Your machine refuses to boot from the CD, so you must use the four-disk set of installation diskettes. Because this is a lab, I'll carry it a step further. Nobody knows where the setup diskettes are, so you need to make your own.

As if this writing, it is still safe to say that most network environments still have a number of systems with Windows 98 installed. If this is not the case, there are a number of Web sites that offer boot disk images that you can download. Here's how to create a boot disk on a Windows 98 machine.

1. Open the Control Panel. This can be done by either right-clicking My Computer and clicking Properties, and then double-clicking the Control Panel icon; or you can click Start>Settings>Control Panel.

2. In Control Panel, double-click Add/Remove Programs. The right-hand tab at the top says Startup Disk. Click that tab, make sure that there is a blank, formatted high-density floppy diskette in the drive, and click Create Disk. You now have the necessary tools for booting a computer to a command prompt.

   NOTE: Windows installation files are stored in *cabinet files,* usually referred to simply as cab files. Each cab file contains large numbers of smaller files that have been compressed together. Many administrators copy the cab files to the hard disk after installation to prevent the need for having the CD-ROM available every time a change has to be made to the computer. If you happen to have a machine that does not have the cab files installed, Setup will prompt you for the Windows 98 CD.

EXERCISE 1 DISCUSSION

1. If you were going to be dealing with operating systems such as Windows 2000,

why would you need a boot diskette made by an earlier operating system?

2. Why do you need the Windows 98 CD to create a boot diskette if the cab files are not installed? And what are cab files?

EXERCISE 2: CREATING THE WINDOWS 2000 BOOT DISK SET

1. Using the boot diskette you just created (or were supplied), start your machine with the diskette in the drive. Select the option Start computer with CD-ROM support and let the machine boot. If your machine will not boot the floppy, it is most likely that your CMOS simply needs to be configured accordingly. Consult with your instructor for the appropriate methods for configuring the CMOS on your particular machine.

2. Once the machine boots, it will tell you what drive letter it assigned to the CD-ROM drive. With the WIN98 Startup Diskette, assuming that there is only one hard drive, this is usually E. This is because the startup diskette creates a virtual drive in memory onto which it copies certain files.

3. From this point on, I will assume the CD-ROM to be Drive E. If this is not the case on your particular system, simply substitute the appropriate drive letter whenever Drive E is referenced. Now you are ready to begin installation.

4. Log onto the CD-ROM by typing E: <Enter>. Confirm you're on the right drive by typing dir <Enter>.

5. At the E: prompt, type CD bootdisk <Enter>.

6. At the E:\bootdisk prompt, type `makeboot` <Enter>. Have four blank, formatted high-density floppy diskettes ready. You will be prompted to enter what drive the diskette is in. Make sure that one of the diskettes is in Drive A and press the <A> key. This becomes your Installation Boot Diskette. Once this diskette is complete, you will be prompted to insert diskettes 2, 3, and finally 4. To avoid confusion, label the diskettes as you go.

EXERCISE 2 DISCUSSION

1. If Windows 2000 ships on a bootable CD, why do you need installation diskettes?

2. Why does the Windows 98 boot diskette not automatically load the CD-ROM drive as D (or the next letter up from your last hard drive if more than one are installed)?

3. In what directory on the CD is the utility that makes a set of installation diskettes located?

4. What happens if your diskettes are not properly formatted before using them for installation diskettes?

EXERCISE 3: INSTALLING WINDOWS 2000 PROFESSIONAL

1. Place the Installation Boot Diskette into Drive A and reboot the machine.

   NOTE: Some schools are provided special versions of Windows 2000 for educational purposes. If you are using the 120-day Evaluation (For Educational Use) or the MSDN CD provided by Microsoft, the I386 directory, which contains the installation files, might be a subdirectory buried elsewhere on the CD. If this is the case, your instructor will have the appropriate information.

2. Once POST has been completed, you will get a screen that says that Setup is detecting your hardware. This is a program called NTDETECT. Setup then begins copying files to memory. You will be prompted for each diskette as it is needed. This is known as the *text-based* portion of Setup.

3. Toward the end of copying diskette 4, you will get a message at the bottom of the screen that says "Setup is starting Windows 2000." This process may take a few moments. Eventually, you will come to a blue screen with cyan letters, save for the top heading that says "Welcome to Setup" in white letters. Read and note the options available, then press <Enter>. If you are using Microsoft's 120-day evaluation copy, you will be presented with a screen advising you of this fact.

4. Read very carefully every single word of the eight-page licensing agreement and then press <F8> to continue. You will now see a screen that details each physical drive installed on your system and any partitions that exist. Your lab machines should show unused space equal to the size of the drive installed. You want to create two partitions. Highlight the unused space and press <C> to create a partition.

5. Make your first partition equal to fifty percent of the available space and continue.

6. On the next screen, select Convert the partition to NTFS and press <Enter>. The next screen simply confirms that you really want to convert the file system. Press <C> to convert. The installation program will then format the drive.

NOTE: During the initial formatting process, the hard drive will be formatted to FAT, even if you selected NTFS as your file system of choice. If you are creating a file system of 2GB or larger, the installation program will automatically format the drive to FAT32. Any partition smaller than 2GB will be formatted in FAT16.

7. Next, the file copy process will begin. This can take quite some time, depending on the speed of your CD-ROM and disk drives. When the files have been copied, you will be prompted to remove all disks from your drives and reboot the computer.

8. On reboot, you enter the graphical portion of the installation process. The Windows 2000 Professional logo will appear. At the bottom a progress bar labeled Starting up will appear.

9. After that, Setup will convert the drive to NTFS. This takes a minute or two. The computer will automatically reboot once again.

10. Setup will now perform a thorough Plug 'n Play (PnP) scan, looking for any PnP devices and/or legacy devices previously installed on a prior OS (in the case of an upgrade). If your screen appears to flicker and Setup halts for a few minutes, this is normal. If Setup halts for an abnormally long time, it is probably hung up and you will need to restart your machine once again.

11. When this is finished, you'll have the opportunity to configure your regional settings. Click Next and type in your name and organization (organization is optional).

12. Now it is time to type in the twenty-five-digit CD key that shipped with the software. Type carefully, or you'll be doing it again.

13. The following screen will provide a suggested NetBIOS computer name. You won't be using its suggestion. Student machines will be named STUDENT1 through STUDENT12 (or however many student machines there are in the classroom). For the password *all* students will simply use *password.* This will avoid the inevitable confusion when someone says, "I forgot what I used."

14. Next you set the time and date, if they are incorrect, and reset the time zone to your own. Setup will default to Pacific Standard.

15. Now you are asked to enter either a domain or workgroup name. Use the workgroup option, accepting the default name.

16. Setup will now begin installing networking components, followed by Windows 2000 components. Let everything install as per default.

17. In the final step, the installation program installs the Start Menu, registers components, saves settings, and finally removes any temporary files used. Click Finish to reboot.

18. When your computer reboots once again, if there are any hardware devices that were detected for which Windows did not have a correct device driver in its database, you will be prompted to search for the appropriate drivers. At this point the drivers can be anywhere, including the network, if networking was configured for DHCP and there is a DHCP server available.

EXERCISE 3 DISCUSSION

1. Explain the purpose and functions of POST.

2. What does NTDETECT do?

3. What happens if you decline Microsoft's generous licensing agreement?

4. At what point does Windows 2000 Setup actually convert your hard drive to NTFS?

5. What happens if you incorrectly type in the twenty-five-digit key, or if you don't have one to type in?

EXERCISE 4: CONNECTING CLIENT TO SERVER

Next, you will pretend you have other types of servers on your network and go through the procedures of installing the appropriate client.

The procedure for adding a client is the same for all; therefore, you will add a Novell client.

1. Right-click My Network Places and select Properties. This will bring up the Network and Dial-up Connections screen illustrated in **Figure 2.1**.

2. Right-click Local Area Connection and select Properties. This brings up, coincidentally enough, the Local Area Connection Properties screen (**Figure 2.2**).

3. Click Install and highlight Client. Click Add.

4. From the following screen select Gateway (and Client) services for NetWare.

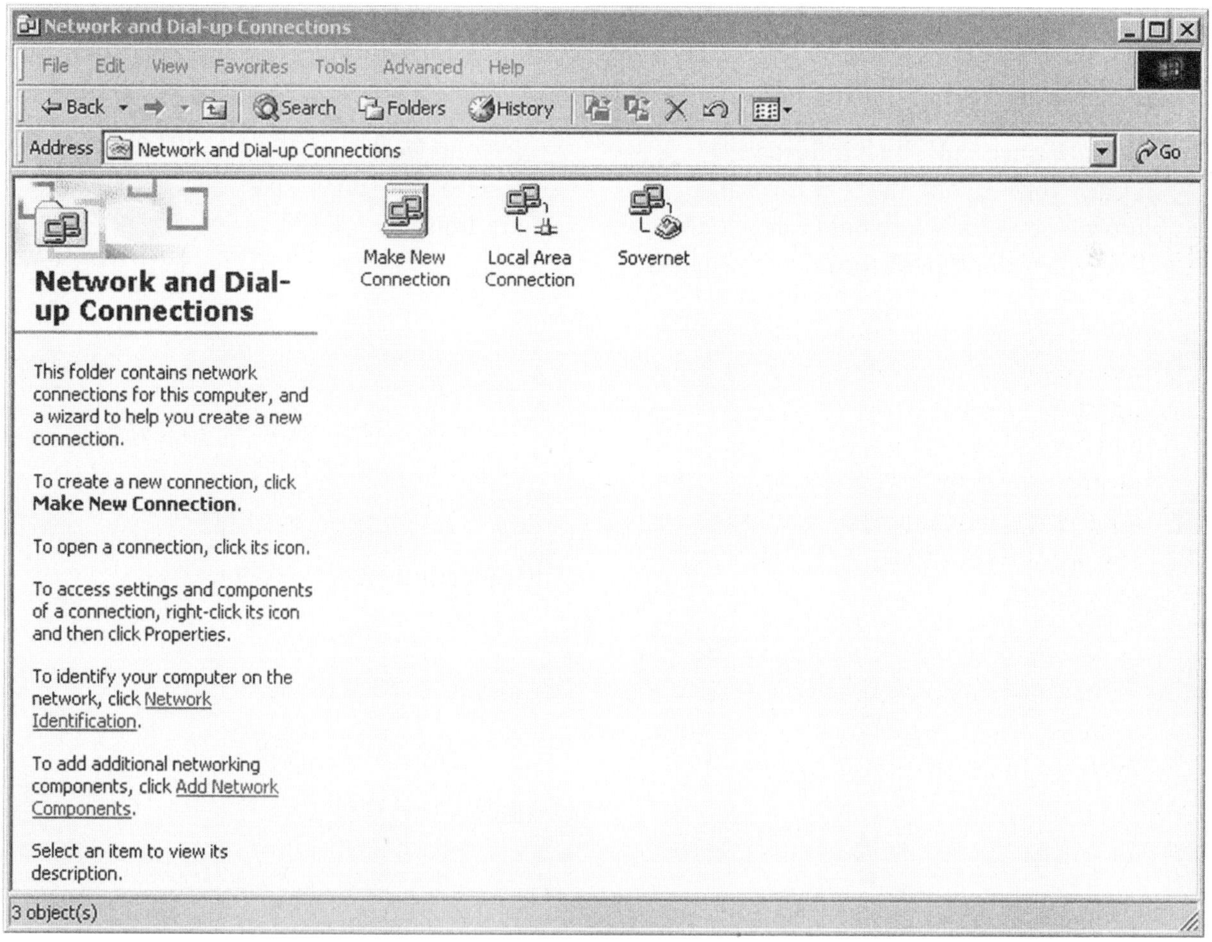

Figure 2.1 Network and Dial-up Connections in Windows 2000

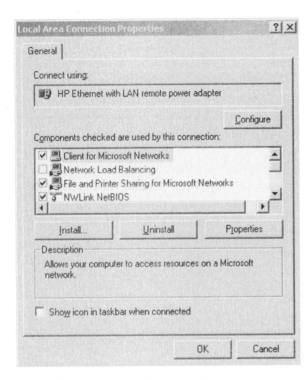

Figure 2.2 Local Area Connection Properties   **Figure 2.3** Configuring the client

5. You will now be asked to configure the client (**Figure 2.3**). The information needed to complete this screen is all information that you would have configured when the Novell server was installed, so you cannot complete this exercise in a network with no Novell servers. Therefore, simply click Cancel. You are finished.

NETWORK TOPOLOGY

INTRODUCTION

The next set of exercises is primarily going to be mental. You are going to diagram three different networks, using three different topologies.

MATERIALS

The only tools or special items you're going to need are:

- Pencils and paper
- Your textbooks
- An alert mind

NOTE: In the textbook, follow along in Chapter One, Some Raw Basics of Networking.

NETWORK+ EXAM OBJECTIVES COVERED IN THIS LAB

1.1 Recognize the different logical or physical network topologies given a diagram, schematic or description.

1.2 Specify the main features of 802.2 (Logical Link Control), 802.3 (Ethernet),

802.5 (token ring), 802.11 (wireless), and FDDI (Fiber Distributed Data Interface) networking technologies.

1.6 Identify the purposes, features and functions of network components.

EXERCISE 1: TOPOLOGY DESIGN

1. On a sheet of paper, diagram a network containing a server, two printers, and four workstations, using a bus topology. List the different components you'll need to complete the job and different media that could be used, and describe advantages and restrictions.

2. On a sheet of paper, diagram a network containing a server, a switch, one printer, and four workstations, using a star topology. List the different components you'll need to complete the job and different media that could be used, and describe advantages and restrictions.

3. Using the same components listed in Step 1, diagram a typical ring network. List

the different components you'll need to complete the job and different media that could be used, and describe advantages and restrictions.

EXERCISE 1 DISCUSSION

1. Why is your bus network limited to 10Mb/s?

2. Would it be possible to create a star network using coaxial cable? If so, why might you not really want to? If it is not possible, why not?

3. What are two different networking technologies that use a ring topology?

EXERCISE 2: IDENTIFYING TOPOLOGY

Match the following topology diagrams to the correct network.

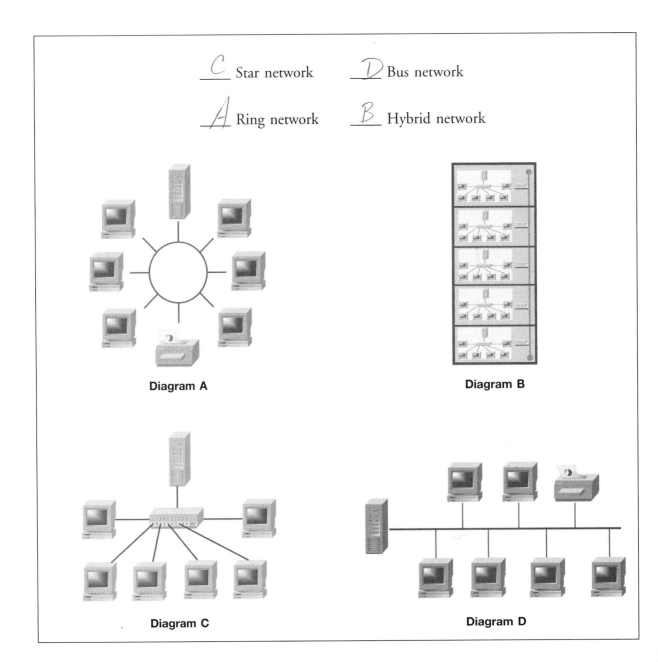

_C_ Star network   _D_ Bus network

_A_ Ring network   _B_ Hybrid network

Diagram A

Diagram B

Diagram C

Diagram D

OPTIONAL EXERCISE: THE MULTILAYERED LAN

1. In this exercise you have been asked to network a company whose offices span a seven-story building. The company wants a separate subnet on each story. Diagram how you will network each floor (using a single floor as an example) and how you can interconnect the floors.

2. List some components that might be useful (or necessary) in order to complete this multifloor network that might not be required of a LAN occupying only a single floor. Explain why you would want to use them.

OPTIONAL EXERCISE DISCUSSION

1. Which of the network topologies best suits the seven-story office building? Is there another way to network this building?

2. In any of the topologies discussed earlier (except the bus) what would be the advantage of using a switch over a router?

SETTING UP A PEER-TO-PEER NETWORK

INTRODUCTION

In the following exercises, you will get your first taste of actually networking multiple devices. You will interconnect the computers onto which you installed Windows 2000 Professional in Lab 2 and hook them all together in a small peer-to-peer (P2P) network. But before you do that, you are going to need to install NICs.

MATERIALS

To complete this lab, you will need several items.

- The student machines

- A NIC with drivers (if necessary) for each machine

- Technician's tool kits

- The patch cables you made in Lab 1

- A hub

NETWORK+ EXAM OBJECTIVES COVERED IN THIS LAB

1.6 Identify the purposes, features and functions of network components.

2.6 Identify classful IP (Internet Protocol) ranges and their subnet masks (For example: Class A, B and C).

3.2 Identify the basic capabilities needed for client workstations to connect to and use network resources.

EXERCISE 1: INSTALLING A NIC

1. Place the computer on the desk in front of you. Depending on the model, you will either need to remove the case or the access panel in order to add components. Since the methods for doing this vary greatly from one model of computer to another, it isn't practical to provide

instructions on how to open the computer in this text. If you are unclear on how to open your computer, consult with your instructor.

2. Now it's time to read any instructions that come with your NIC. Some brands, such as 3-Com, require that you run a small setup program before installing the NIC, while others have you install the driver after the card is in place.

3. Find a free PCI slot and remove the backplane cover for that slot (see **Figure 4.1**). Firmly seat the NIC into the slot and replace the backplane screw.

4. Start the computer and let Plug 'n Play do its thing. With Windows 2000, the NIC should automatically be detected. Depending on your card and the installation process used, PnP will either identify the card and find the appropriate driver in its database or it won't. If you ran a setup program such as 3-Com's prior to installing the card, that setup added the appropriate drivers to the database. If no driver is found by PnP, during the installation process you will get a screen like the one in **Figure 4.2**, followed by the one in **Figure 4.3**. Specify the appropriate location of the disk containing your drivers and click Next.

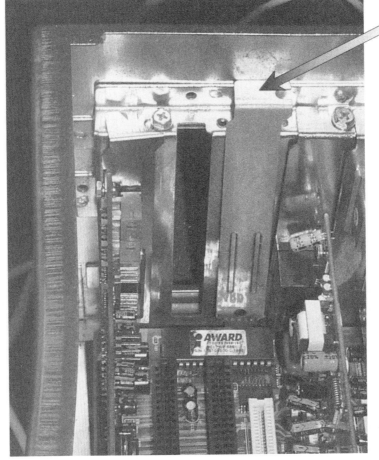

Backplane cover

Figure 4.1 The backplane cover (raised in this illustration) is actually an essential part of your computer's thermal regulation system. Any time you remove a card, fill the open slot with a cover.

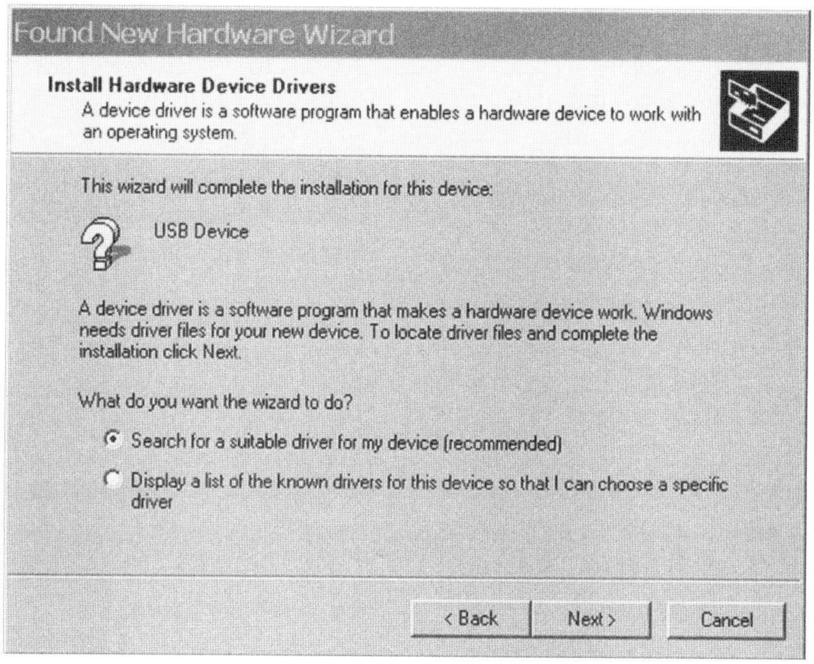

Figure 4.2 In most circumstances, it is best to let Windows search for a device driver. Select that option for this lab.

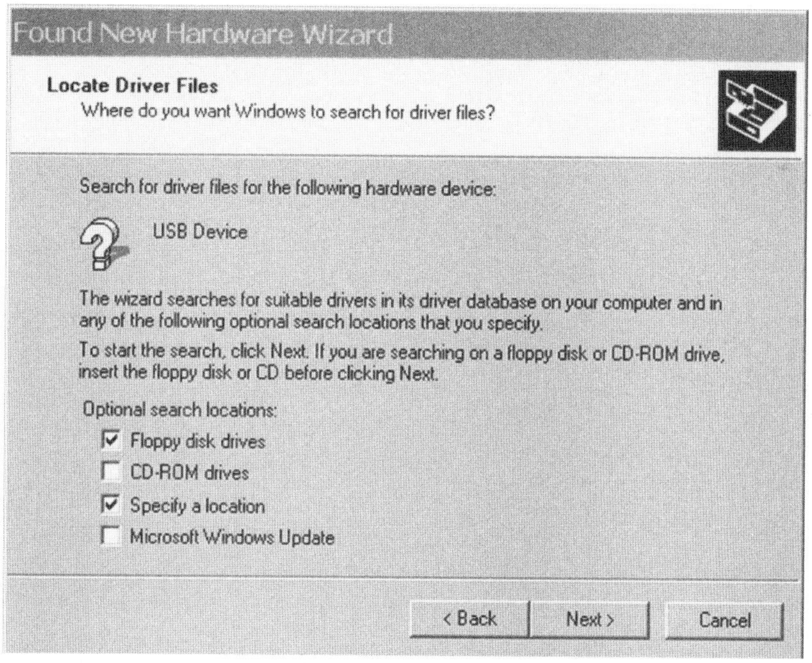

Figure 4.3 Click the appropriate box that specifies where your driver is located. To save a little time, deselect everything else.

5. If you get a screen warning you that the driver does not contain a Microsoft signature, don't worry about that. Continue the installation and let the driver install. Depending on the brand of NIC and its drivers, you may or may not have to restart your computer once again.

6. Your NIC installation is complete.

EXERCISE 1 DISCUSSION

1. Did your NIC require loading a device driver through an installation routine, or was Plug 'n Play able to detect it?

2. What is the purpose of a Microsoft Driver Signature?

EXERCISE 2: CONFIGURING THE PROTOCOLS

After installing a NIC driver, there are certain networking functions that Windows automatically installs. By default, you have installed a networking client in Client for Microsoft Networks. Windows also installs File and Printer Sharing for Microsoft Networks and Internet Protocol (TCP/IP). TCP/IP is configured to automatically obtain an IP address from a DHCP server. Therefore, your machine is configured as a DHCP client as well. Now you are going to change some of that.

STEP 1: RECONFIGURING TCP/IP

The first thing you will do is to statically assign IP addresses to each machine on the network.

1. Right-click My Network Places on the desktop, or click Start>Settings>Network and Dial-up Connections. Either way, you will get to the screen in **Figure 4.4**.

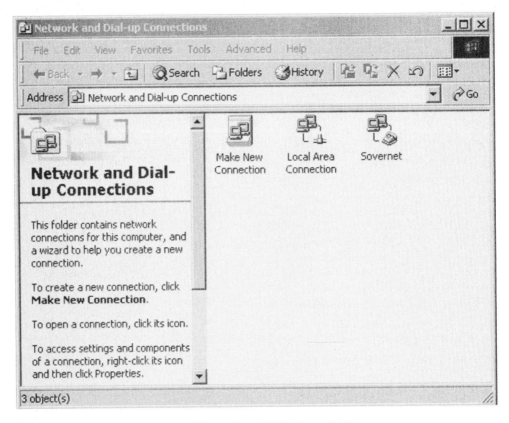

Figure 4.4 Network and Dial-up Connections in Windows 2000

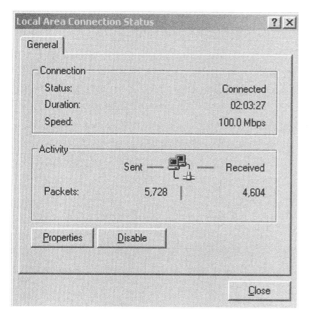

Figure 4.5 Windows 2000 lets you manage all NICs and Dial-up Connections from the same console.

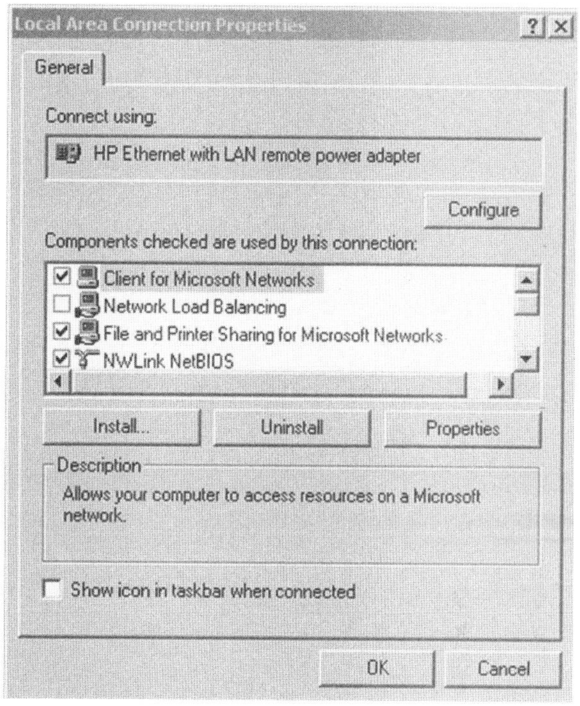

Figure 4.6 Configuring Network Properties in Windows 2000

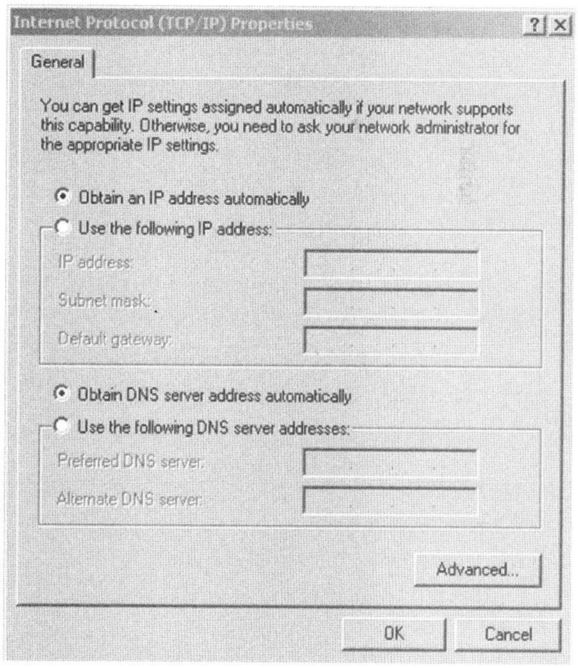

2. Double-click Local Area Connection. The screen shown in **Figure 4.5** will appear. Click Properties.

3. Now you will have the screen shown in **Figure 4.6**. Scroll down to Internet Protocol (TCP/IP) and click Properties.

4. The screen in **Figure 4.7** will be the next thing you see.

5. You will statically configure each of the machines in the classroom. To do this, click on Use the following IP address: and type in the address assigned to your machine. You will derive the address by starting in the front left corner of the classroom and move left to right and then to the back, one row at a time. Start with the IP address of 192.168.1.100 for the first machine. The next machine would be 192.168.1.101, followed by 192.168.1.102, and so on and so forth. Make sure no two machines are inadvertently assigned duplicate addresses. This will cause a conflict. Type in a subnet mask of 255.255.255.0. If you simply

Figure 4.7 Managing TCP/IP Settings

press Tab after entering your IP address, the Subnet mask field should fill in automatically. Click OK, and then on the next screen click Close.

STEP 2: CREATING A WORKGROUP

1. Click Start>Settings>Control Panel, then double-click System or right-click My Computer and select Properties. Either way will get you to the screen illustrated in **Figure 4.8**.

2. Click the Network Identification tab and then click Properties on the following screen. It will now look similar to **Figure 4.9**. Make sure Workgroup is selected and type in CLASSROOM. Everybody needs to

be in the same workgroup to be part of a P2P network. Therefore, if you type it incorrectly, you won't join the network.

3. Congratulations. You are all now part of the CLASSROOM workgroup. You should be able to see the CLASSROOM workgroup in My Network Places. If you double-click this icon, you should be able to see each other's machines. Note, however, that you won't be able to see any of the contents of these machines as of yet.

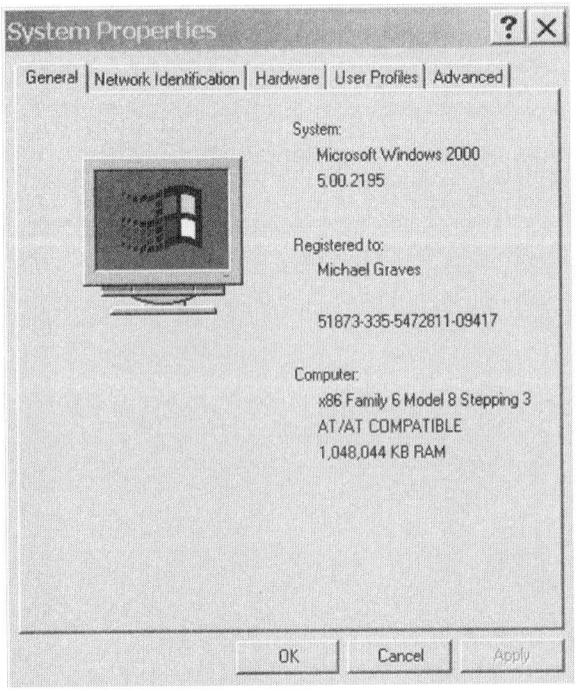

Figure 4.8 The Windows 2000 Control Panel is very similar to earlier versions.

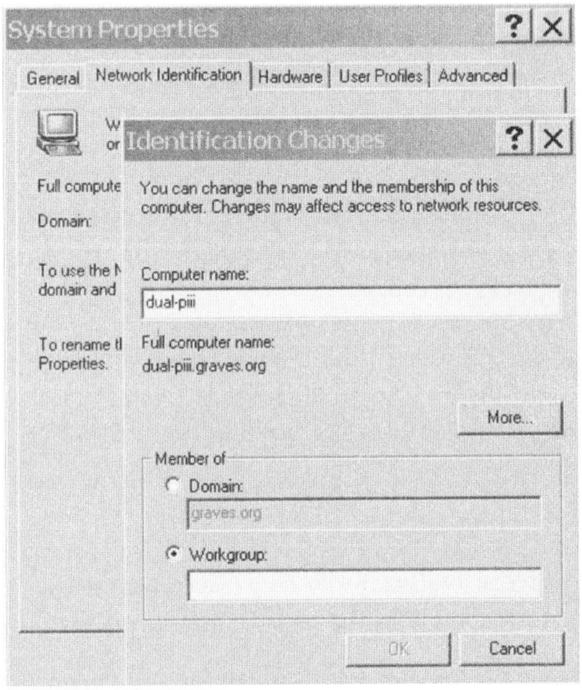

Figure 4.9 The Network Identification setting is the same as your NetBIOS name. In earlier versions of Windows, this would be found in Network Properties.

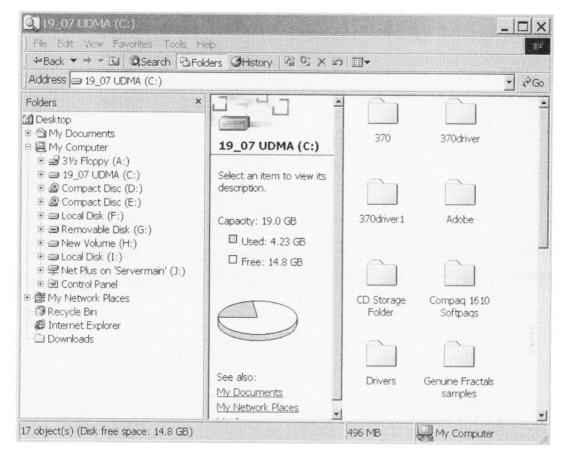

Figure 4.10 Resource sharing and security is managed from Windows Explorer.

STEP 3: SHARING RESOURCES

1. Right-click the Start button and select Explore. This will open Windows Explorer, as shown in **Figure 4.10**. You are going to create a new folder in which you can store your shared files.

2. Highlight Drive C in the left-hand pane. Select the File menu, New, and then Folder. Give the folder your first name.

3. When the new folder appears in the left-hand pane, right-click that folder and in the pull-down menu that appears, one of the options will be Sharing. Click that option. The screen illustrated in **Figure 4.11** will appear.

4. Select Share this folder and leave the default share name in place. Don't worry if more than one of you have the same

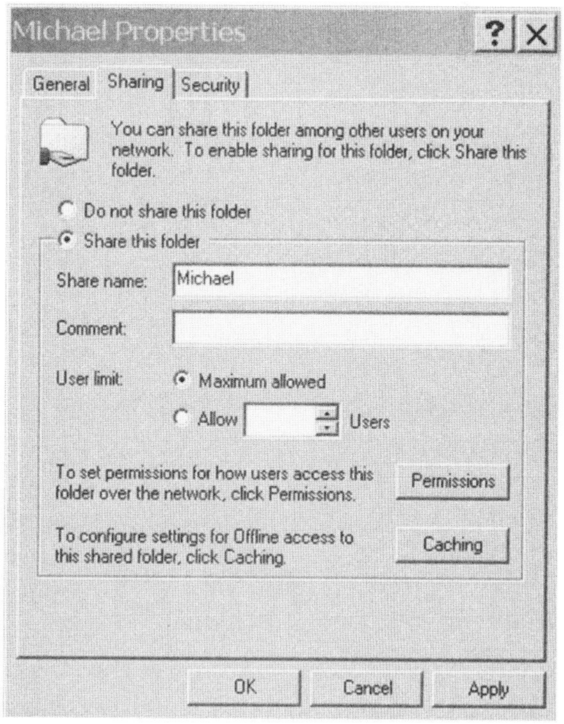

Figure 4.11 Sharing options in Windows 2000

first name. Just don't try to put two shared folders with the same share name on the same computer. You won't worry about permissions in this lab, so simply click Apply and then OK.

5. Now, in the left pane of Windows Explorer, double-click your shared folder. The right-hand pane should be empty. Right-click anywhere in that pane and you'll get a pop-up menu. Select New, and then in the next menu that appears, select Text Document.

6. Type the following text. "My house is brown, but my horse is yellow." Don't worry about how stupid that sounds. One of your classmates is going to fix that for you. Close the document and when it prompts you to save the file, save it as house.txt.

7. Now everybody pick a teammate. (Pick somebody you don't know so that you can learn to work together at the same time and maybe make a new friend.) In Windows Explorer, double-click My Network Places and browse to your partner's machine. Open the file and edit it to read, "My house is yellow, but my horse is brown." Save the file and close it.

8. Once you're both finished, you should be able to open your version of house.txt and see the revisions your partner made.

EXERCISE 3: INSTALLING A NETWORK CLIENT

Of course, Microsoft is not the only manufacturer of NOSs in the world. There are several others every bit as good, and for certain applications, possibly considered better. You might need to connect your work station to a Novell or a Unix server. In the following exercise, you will see how to install the Novell client.

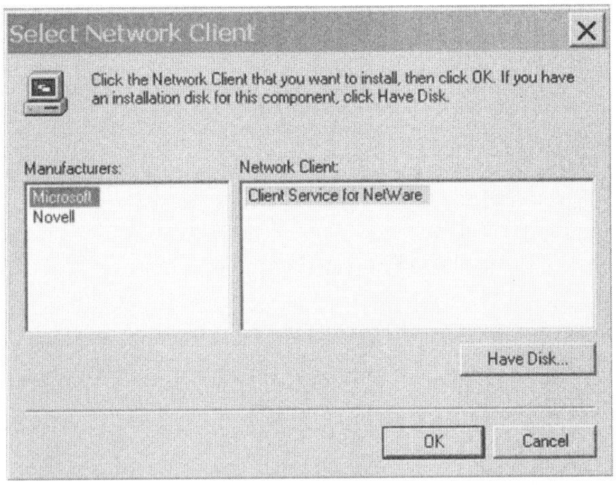

Figure 4.12 Windows 2000 provides network clients for Microsoft and Novell networks. For Unix and Linux networks, you will have to have the appropriate files on either floppy disks, CD, or a known network location and then select Have Disk.

1. Return to your Local Area Connection Properties screen and click Install. On the Network Component Type screen, select Client and click Add. This will bring up the screen in **Figure 4.12**.

2. Click Microsoft and select Client Services for NetWare. Click OK. Your machine will think about it for a couple of seconds and then prompt you to restart your machine.

3. In order to install Unix, Linux, or other networking client software, you would need to have the files stored somewhere on the network, on floppy diskette, or on CD. You would then click the Have Disk option.

OPTIONAL LAB 1: DUAL-HOMING A COMPUTER

In order to perform this lab, you will need a second NIC for each computer. Each NIC will be configured to work on a separate network.

STEP 1: INSTALLING THE NIC

This is easy. Simply repeat Exercise 1 of this lab, step-by-step. There are no variations.

STEP 2: CONFIGURING THE PROTOCOLS

Repeat Exercise 2 of this lab. However, when you get to Procedure 5, instead of starting your series of IP addresses at 192.168.1.100, start with 192.168.10.100.

Now when you open Network and Dial-up Connections, you will see an icon for Local Area Connection 1 and Local Area Connection 2. Each one can be independently configured. You now have two networks running simultaneously in the classroom.

Have half the classroom reconfigure their Network Identification in the System Properties screen so that they are members of a workgroup called WORKGROUP. You will have to restart these machines for the change to take effect. Now, in My Network Places, you should be able to browse to both workgroups.

INSTALLING A NETWORK OPERATING SYSTEM

INTRODUCTION

This lab takes you through the first stages of creating a client-server network, which is the installation and configuration of a network operating system (NOS) onto a computer. Once this is done, regardless of any hardware that may be installed later, the computer is effectively a server.

There are a number of excellent NOSs available on the market put out by companies such as Novell, Unix, Citrix, and Microsoft. An excellent example of a virtually free NOS is Linux. Unfortunately, time and space prohibit me from describing (and you from performing) a complete installation of each and every one. You will be installing Microsoft's Windows 2000 Server (W2KS) in the following lab.

MATERIALS

For these exercises, each student will need the following equipment:

- A computer configured to boot to CD-ROM (or a working W2K Professional or Windows 98 machine)

- A Windows 2000 Server CD

- Four blank, formatted 3.5" 1.44MB floppy diskettes

NETWORK+ EXAM OBJECTIVES COVERED IN THIS LAB

2.13 Identify the purpose of network services and protocols.

3.1 Identify the basic capabilities (For example: client support, interoperability, authentication, file and print services, application support and security) of the server operating systems to access network resources.

4.6 Given a scenario, determine the impact of modifying, adding or removing network services.

EXERCISE 1: CREATING A SET OF INSTALLATION DISKETTES

If you are using retail versions of W2KS in your classroom, the package shipped with the CD and a set of four installation diskettes for installing onto systems that cannot boot from a CD.

However, as everyone knows all too well, diskettes are easily lost or corrupted. Therefore, you will start with the creation of new diskettes.

1. The first step is to open the Makebt32 application. How you do this depends on the setup you are using.

   If you are booting from a CD insert the W2K Server (W2KS) CD into the CD-ROM drive and boot the machine. Once the machine boots to a command prompt, type `cd bootdisk`. At the command prompt, type `makeboot`.

   If you are running an active machine, insert the W2KS CD into the drive. If Autorun is configured on your machine, you will get a screen similar to the one in **Figure 5.1**. Select Browse This CD. Double-click the BOOTDISK icon, then double-click the MAKEBT32 icon.

2. With either of the above methods, you should get a screen like the one shown in **Figure 5.2**.

3. Insert the first of your blank, formatted floppy diskettes into the floppy drive and type a. The first diskette will be your first boot diskette. As the diskette creation process continues, the application will prompt you as it needs the additional diskettes.

4. When the final diskette is complete the window will close. Carefully label your diskettes and store them someplace safe.

EXERCISE 1 DISCUSSION

1. What is the purpose of creating boot diskettes if the CD itself is bootable?

2. What will happen if, during the disk creation process, you insert a diskette with data already on it?

EXERCISE 2: INSTALLING A NOS

The actual procedure for installing W2KS is not much different that that of installing W2K Pro. The real differences between the two installations will be seen in Lab Six. In order to complete

Figure 5.1 The Autorun screen from W2KS

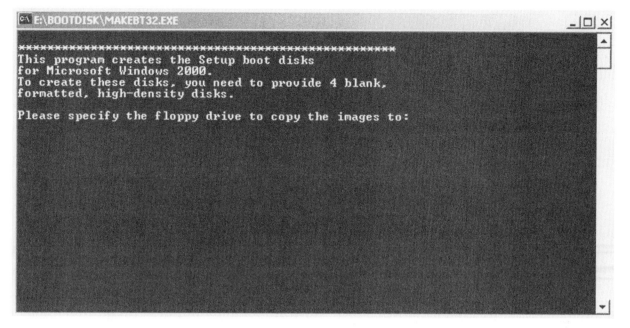

```
E:\BOOTDISK\MAKEBT32.EXE
*****************************************************
This program creates the Setup boot disks
for Microsoft Windows 2000.
To create these disks, you need to provide 4 blank,
formatted, high-density disks.

Please specify the floppy drive to copy the images to:
```

Figure 5.2 Whichever route you take to get here, you'll end up at a command prompt for making your installation diskettes.

some of the later labs you need to be able to create dual-boot machines. By this, I mean that you need the student machines to be able to boot to either W2K Pro or W2KS. Therefore, in this lab, you will install the server product over W2K Pro from the Pro interface. For this exercise, you will need the W2K Pro machines you configured in Lab Two, Installing an Operating System, and a copy of W2KS.

1. Insert the W2KS CD into the drive and wait for the screen shown in **Figure 5.3**. Select Install Windows 2000. Here, you will be informed that W2KS does not support upgrading from W2K Pro. Click OK.

2. The only option you'll have on the next screen is to install a new copy of Windows 2000. Click Next, accept the licensing agreement, and click Next again.

3. On the Select Special Options screen, click Next. Setup will now check for available disk space. Since you have no applications currently installed on your machine, you need not check Microsoft's Directory of Applications. Click Next.

Setup will now copy a large number of files to a temporary directory. This shouldn't take long. Your computer will then restart.

4. During the reboot, you will be given a menu offering the option of starting Windows 2000 Professional or Windows 2000 Server Setup. It will automatically select the Server Setup if you do nothing.

5. Next is the Windows 2000 Server Setup screen. Your options are:

    To set up Windows 2000 now, press <Enter>. This performs a fresh installation and is the option you will select.

    To repair a Windows 2000 Installation, press <R>. If you have an emergency repair diskette for an existing server, this can sometimes help you fix a corrupted OS. (Notice I said "sometimes.")

    To quit setup without installing Windows 2000, press <F3>. This aborts the installation.

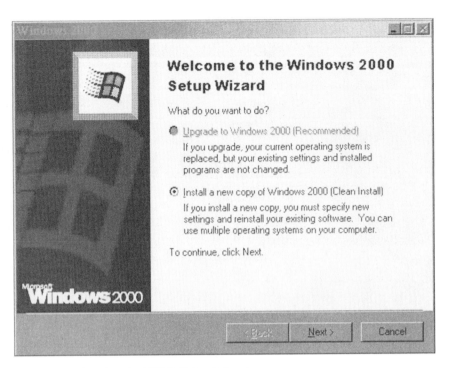

Figure 5.3 Starting the W2KS Setup Wizard

6. Press <Enter>. Now you are prompted to select the partition on which you wish to install your NOS. If you recall, in Lab Two you left half of your hard drive unpartitioned.

7. Highlight your unused partition and press <C> to create a partition. Use all available space and select the NTFS file system. Setup will now format that partition.

8. Next, Setup examines your disks and copies a rather large number of files. This may take a while. Be patient. When the files have been copied your computer will reboot.

9. You'll enter the graphical mode of the setup. The first thing that that happens in this stage is the Plug 'n Play detection of hardware devices. Once the hardware detection has completed, the Regional Settings screen will appear.

10. Click Next. You'll be asked to type in your name and organization. There must

be a value in the name field. Organizational information is optional. Fill in your information and click Next.

11. Enter the product key into the fields provided. Type carefully. Click Next.

12. Now you will be asked to fill in the client licensing information. Your two options are Per Server: number of concurrent connections, and Per Seat. With Per Server licensing, each connection to the server, including the server itself, requires a client license. Per seat, as its name implies, requires a license for each user that is logged on. For the purposes of this lab, enter 50 in the Per Server field and click Next.

13. Next you'll be asked to provide a computer name and an administrator password. Use the same computer name you used in Lab Two. As before, everyone's password should be *password*.

14. On the Windows 2000 Components screen, accept the defaults and click Next.

LAB 5: INSTALLING A NETWORK OPERATING SYSTEM

15. Fill in the Date and Time fields in the next screen if they're not already correct and click Next. Setup will now install Networking Components. Sit back and wait. Accept the default network settings for now—you'll do some tweaking a little later—and click Next.

16. The next screen offers two options, No, this computer is not on a network, and Is on a network without a domain. Select No, this computer is not on a network. Setup will now begin installing components. This can take quite some time, so be patient once again.

17. When this is finished the Final Tasks will be performed. Setup installs Start menu items, registers components, saves settings, and removes any temporary files used.

18. When Setup is finished, you will be prompted to remove any disks from your drives. Click Finish and your computer will reboot. On this reboot, you will be given a text-based menu that offers the option of either Windows 2000 Server or Windows 2000 Professional. By default, you have thirty seconds to make a choice before the highlighted choice, which should be Windows 2000 Server, boots automatically.

19. When the machine has finished rebooting, it will open the Windows 2000 Configure Your Server screen. You will configure this machine in a later lab. Therefore, simply close that screen. W2KS has been successfully installed.

EXERCISE 2 DISCUSSION

Once the NOS was installed, on the final reboot, you had the choice of two different operating systems to which you could start your machine.

1. What file controls these options?

2. What is the default delay for selecting an OS during the boot process? How would you change this?

An Exercise in Encapsulation

Introduction

In the following exercise, you will produce a 3D model of how a stream of data is broken down into frames and how each layer adds the header information. Keep in mind that what you are doing here is representational and not an actual reproduction of a frame.

Materials

Here is what you will need to complete this exercise:

- A roll of cash register or adding machine tape
- Four #10 envelopes for each student
- Three #10 envelopes for the instructor
- Pens or pencils
- A vivid imagination

Network+ Exam Objectives Covered in this Lab

2.1 Identify a MAC (Media Access Control) address and its parts.

2.2 Identify the seven layers of the OSI (Open Systems Interconnect) model and their functions.

Exercise 1: Creating the Data Stream

1. Pull off a strip of adding machine tape about two feet long (longer if you have a large class). The instructor or a volunteer can fill one side of the tape with a message long enough to equal one word for each student in class. Leave room for trimming the words off. Lay the tape out on the instructor's desk.

2. Now it is time to decide two things— what protocol are you going to use, and what kind of file is this going to be? For this exercise you will transfer a JPEG file using FTP.

3. The instructor will now write TCP and LOGON AUTHENTICATED onto one envelope and label that envelope APPLICATION. On a second envelope, write ASCII and PRESENTATION. On a third envelope, write the label SESSION.

Also on this envelope, the instructor will write 1000ms, RPC, and "When you acknowledge, I'll send."

4. Staple or tape these three envelopes to the strip of cash register tape with the message and send it around the room. The students should trim off one word from the strip and place it in one of their envelopes. Pass the strip to the next person.

5. On the envelope into which you put your portion of cash register tape, copy the information from each of the envelopes the instructor provided, identifying it with the appropriate layer. Now, the first student should write 00000001 on his or her envelope, the next should write 00000002 on his or hers, and then 00000003 for the next person, and so on down the line. In addition, write "512 x 16" and then "8192." Now write PORT 20 and label that envelope TRANSPORT.

6. Fold this envelope and place it into another envelope. On the outside of this envelope, write 192.168.0.110. This envelope should be labeled NETWORK.

7. Have somebody go to a computer and type ping 192.168.0.110 from a command prompt. After the echo replies return from the machine, type arp —a. This will give you the MAC address of 192.168.0.110. Write it on the board.

8. Each student can now fold the envelope labeled NETWORK and put it into another envelope and label that one DATA LINK. Write down the MAC address from the blackboard. Underneath that, write "Fast Ethernet", and beneath that write "1024 x 32" followed by "32768."

9. On the outside of your last envelope, write "8192 bits at 1180mv." Label that envelope PHYSICAL.

EXERCISE 1 DISCUSSION

1. What was the purpose of the first envelope labeled APPLICATION that the instructor provided? What other services aside from those illustrated in the lab does this layer provide?

2. What was the purpose of the second envelope labeled PRESENTATION that the instructor provided? What other services aside from those illustrated in the lab does this layer provide?

3. What was the purpose of the third envelope labeled SESSION that the instructor provided? What other services aside from those illustrated in the lab does this layer provide?

   NOTE: It should be pointed out that, in reality, TCP/IP protocols do not make use of session numbers in their headers. TCP/IP has its own method for keeping track of what data goes with what sessions. In this exercise, I used the session numbers to clarify the purpose of each layer. Sequencing information, however, is provided by TCP/IP.

4. Why did you clip off strips from the cash register tape?

5. On the TRANSPORT envelope, what was the purpose of the equation and the associated value? Why do you have the eight-digit numbers on each envelope? What other services aside from those illustrated in the lab does this layer provide? What purpose does the port number serve?

6. Why did you write an IP address on the outside of the NETWORK envelope? What other services aside from those illustrated in the lab does this layer provide?

7. What purpose does the MAC address on the DATA LINK envelope serve, and can

you explain the equation and its answer? What other services aside from those illustrated in the lab does this layer provide?

8. On the outside of the PHYSICAL envelope, you wrote down a hypothetical value of how many bits was contained in the envelope and signified a voltage. Explain this. What other services aside from those illustrated in the lab does this layer provide?

EXERCISE 2: DE-ENCAPSULATION OF A PACKET

1. Have somebody go to the computer again, and at a command prompt, type `tracert 192.168.0.110`. This will provide the NetBIOS name of the computer at that IP address.

This should indicate the instructor machine.

2. Now, pass the envelopes around the room in a random pattern, making sure they get shuffled around as much as possible. Then pass them up to the instructor's desk.

3. Open the envelopes and use the Session Layer sequence numbers to put the strips of data back into order. Your message should be complete.

EXERCISE 2 DISCUSSION

1. Why did you have to do a Tracert of the IP address before you could locate the instructor machine?

2. Explain what else would be going on during the reassembly process that you did not try to replicate in this exercise. Go over each layer, one at a time.

CONFIGURING A DOMAIN CONTROLLER

INTRODUCTION

In Lab Five, Installing a Network Operating System, you took the first major step in setting up a network server. However, you still have a lot more to do before it becomes a serviceable server. At this point in time, it is simply a stand-alone machine. In this lab, you will configure the server to be a primary domain controller on the network.

For this lab (and some of the ensuing labs) to work properly, the class needs to break up into teams of two. In later labs team members will be alternating between acting as the server and a client machine.

MATERIALS

To complete this lab, you will need the following:

- The machines onto which W2KS was installed in Lab Five

- The W2KS CDs that were used to install the product

NOTE: Information for the following exercises can be found in Chapter Two, The Client/Server Network; Chapter Eleven, An Introduction to TCP/IP; and Chapter Seventeen, Preparing for a Network Installation.

NETWORK+ EXAM OBJECTIVES COVERED IN THIS LAB

2.4 Differentiate between network protocols in terms of routing, addressing schemes, interoperability and naming conventions.

2.5 Identify the components and structure of IP (Internet Protocol) addresses (IPv4, IPv6) and the required setting for connections across the Internet.

2.10 Define the purpose, function and use of protocols used in the TCP/IP (Transmission Control Protocol/Internet Protocol) suite.

3.1 Identify the basic capabilities (For example: client support, interoperability, authentication, file and print services, application support and security) of server operating systems to access network resources.

EXERCISE 1: PROMOTING THE SERVER

Before a machine can be configured to run as a primary domain controller, it must be *promoted*. If you recall, you originally set this machine up

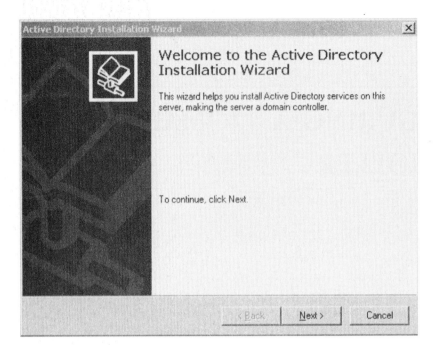

Figure 7.1   The Active Directory Installation Wizard

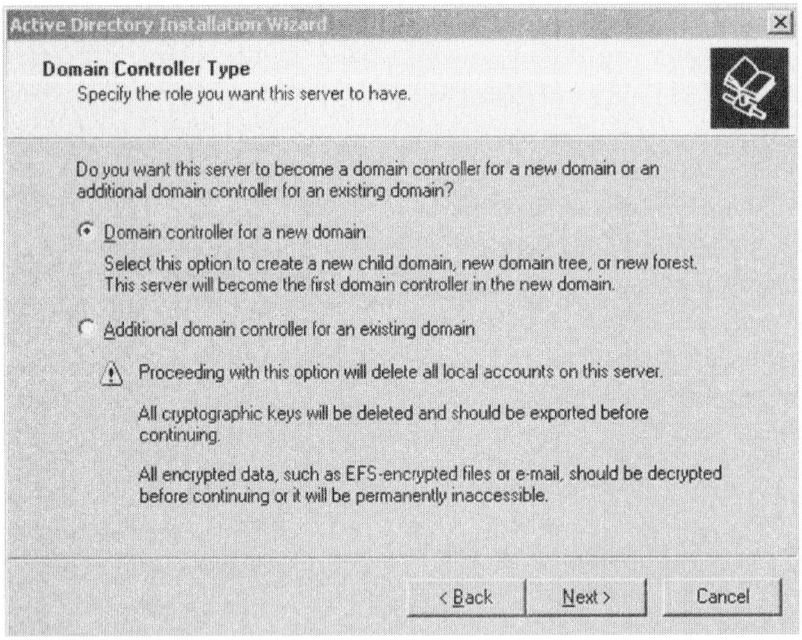

Figure 7.2   Creation of a domain controller

to be off the network. Now you will make it a controller.

1. Click Start>Run and type dcpromo into the command field. This will open the Active Directory Installation Wizard, as shown in **Figure 7.1**. Click Next.

2. The next screen that opens (**Figure 7.2**) offers two options. The first is to create a Domain controller for a new domain. This is the option to select when setting up the first domain controller on a network and is the option you will select. The second option is Additional domain controller for

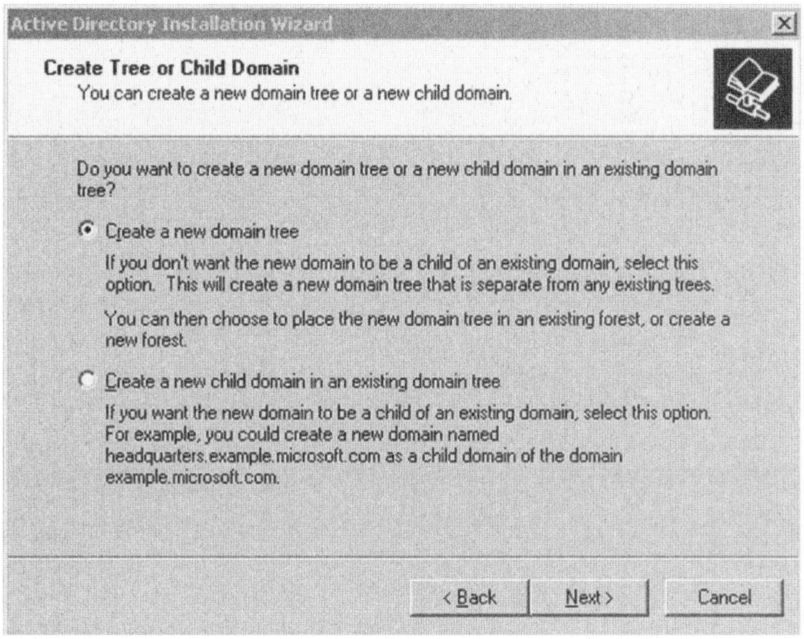

Figure 7.3 Creation of an Active Directory Tree

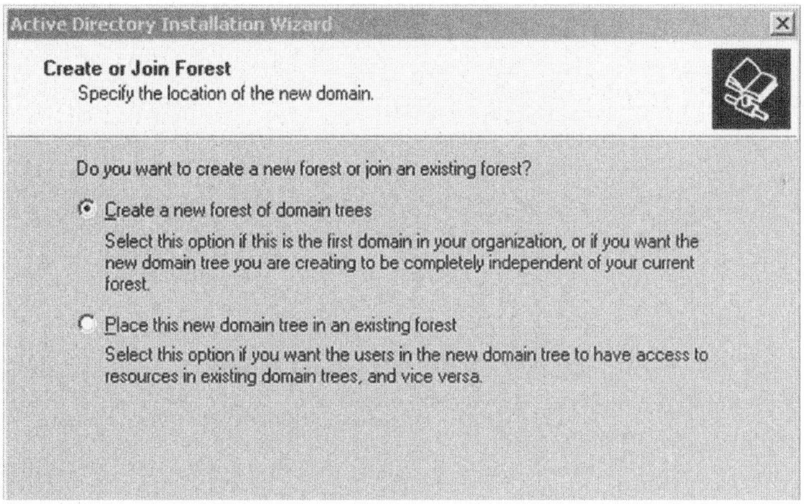

Figure 7.4 Creation of an Active Directory forest

an existing domain. This option allows you to place additional servers on your network or to create a subdomain to an existing network. Click Domain controller for a new domain and then click Next.

3. You will now have a window open labeled Create Tree or Child Domain (**Figure 7.3**). Once again, you have two options. The first is Create a new domain tree. Once

again, this is the option for first servers on the network. The second option, Create a new child domain in an existing domain tree, is used for establishing secondary or subdomains. Click Create a new domain tree and then click Next.

4. The screen that follows is labeled Create or Join Forest (**Figure 7.4**). As with the previous screens, there are two options.

45

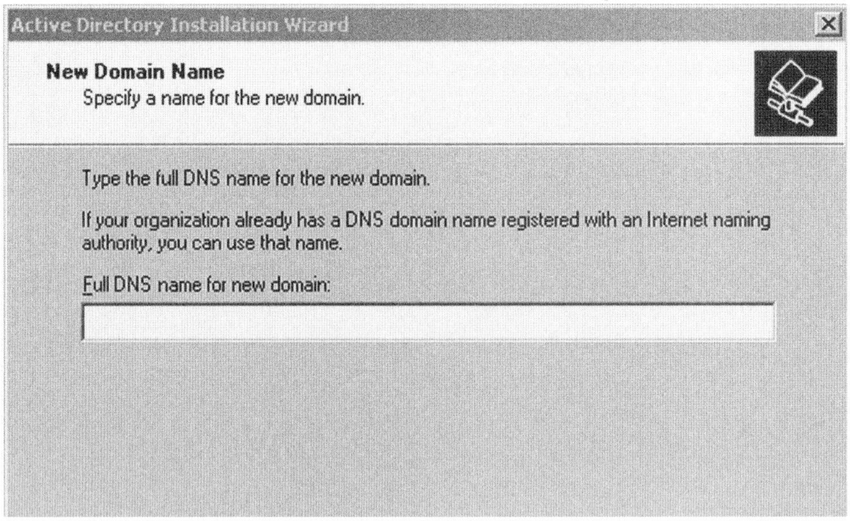

Figure 7.5   Establishing a domain name

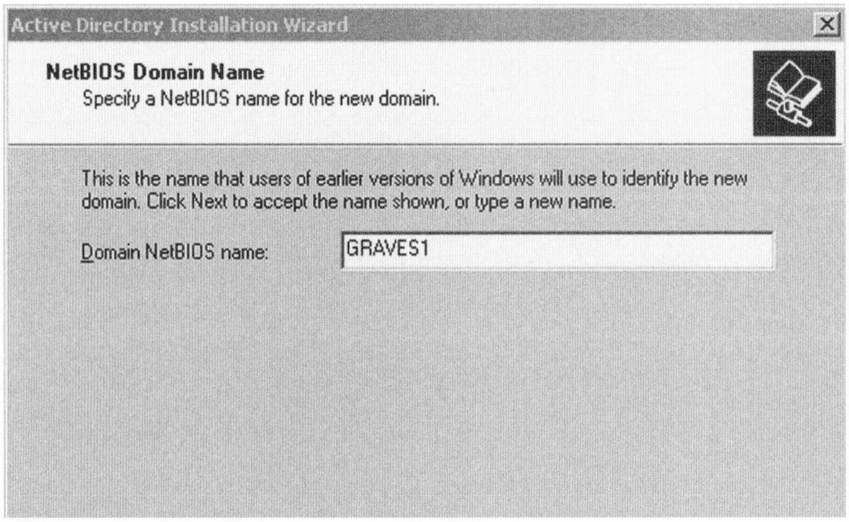

Figure 7.6   Establishing a domain name compatible with pre-Windows 2000 machines

The first is Create a new forest of domain trees. This is the option for new domain controllers. Place this new domain tree in an existing forest is the second option and is used for creating subdomains. Click Create a new forest of domain trees and then Next.

5.   The next screen (**Figure 7.5**) is labeled New Domain Name. Here, you need a DNS-compliant name such as xyz.com. To maintain a semblance of order in our classroom, you will assign domain names

of STUDENT1.ORG, STUDENT2.ORG, STUDENT3.ORG, and so on until each student machine in the classroom is an independent domain. Fill in your domain name and click Next.

6.   Now you will be prompted to either accept a default NetBIOS name for your new domain or to enter a new one that will be compatible with earlier versions of Windows (see **Figure 7.6**). Keep the default name and click Next.

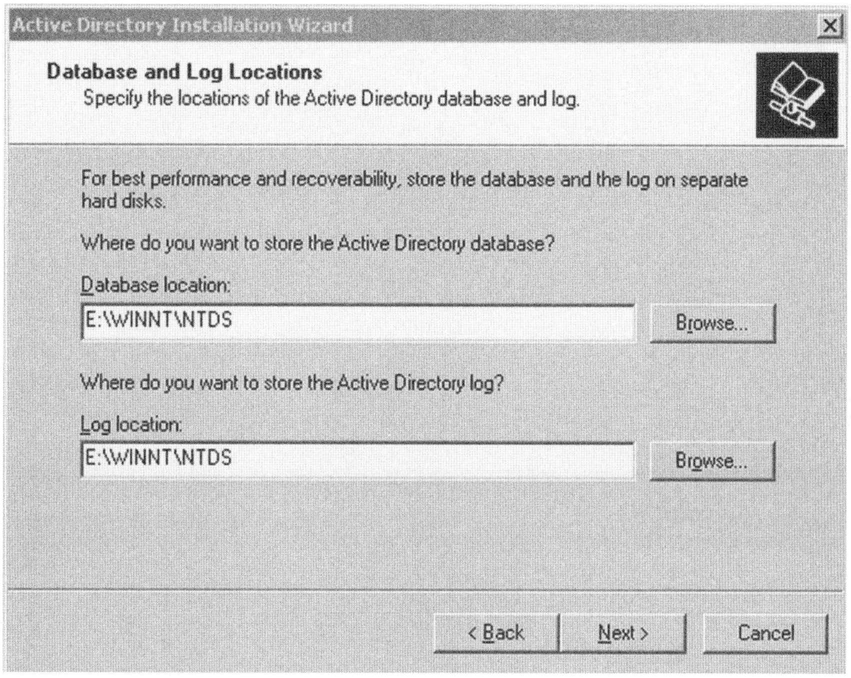

Figure 7.7 Establishing database and log locations

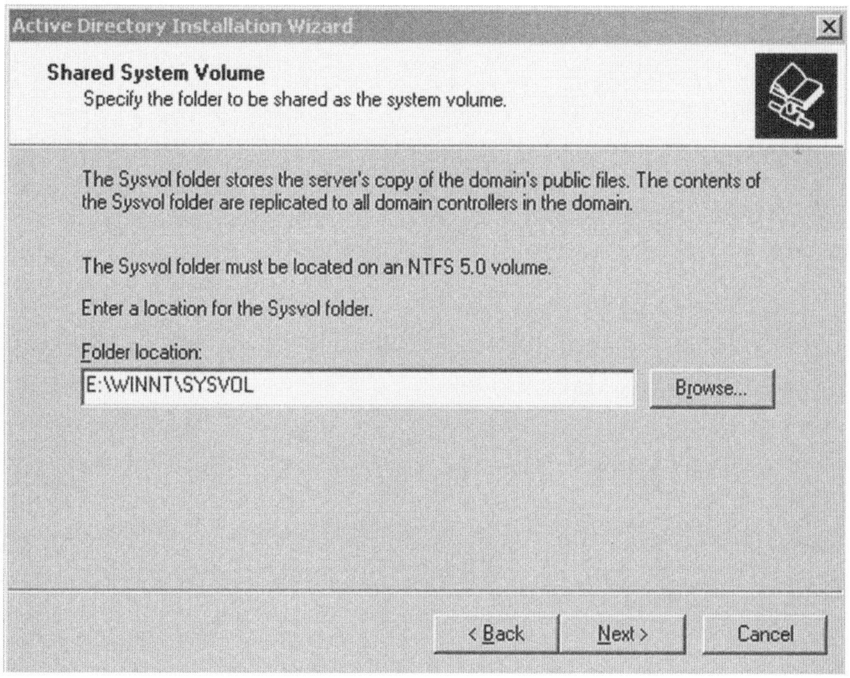

Figure 7.8 Setting the location of the shared system volume

7. The next two screens are Database and Log Locations (**Figure 7.7**) and Shared System Volume (**Figure 7.8**). Accept the default path locations and click Next on each of these two screens.

8. This will cause a pop-up warning to appear (**Figure 7.9**) telling you that a DNS server could not be contacted. Don't worry about this. Simply click OK.

Figure 7.9 This warning is simply telling you that the installation wizard cannot find a DNS server. You will create one in the next step.

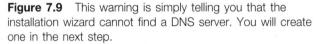

Figure 7.10 Configuring DNS

9. This brings up the Configure DNS screen (**Figure 7.10**). The two options are Yes, install and configure DNS on this computer (recommended) and No. I will install and configure DNS myself. Click Yes, install and configure DNS on this computer (recommended) and then Next.

10. This brings up the Permissions screen (**Figure 7.11**). Déjà vu! You have two options! The first is Permissions compatible with pre-Windows 2000 servers and the second is Permissions compatible only with Windows 2000 servers. You would select the second option *only* if you know beyond any shadow of a doubt that there will never be any earlier versions of Windows NOS installed on any server anywhere on your network, and that there will be no Novell, Unix, or Linux boxes acting as servers now or later on. Make sure that Permissions compatible with pre-Windows 2000 servers is selected and click Next.

11. Next you will be prompted to enter a password for entering Directory Services Restore Mode (**Figure 7.12**). Some administrators use a separate password for this function. For the purposes of these labs, simply enter *password* once again. Confirm your entry and click Next.

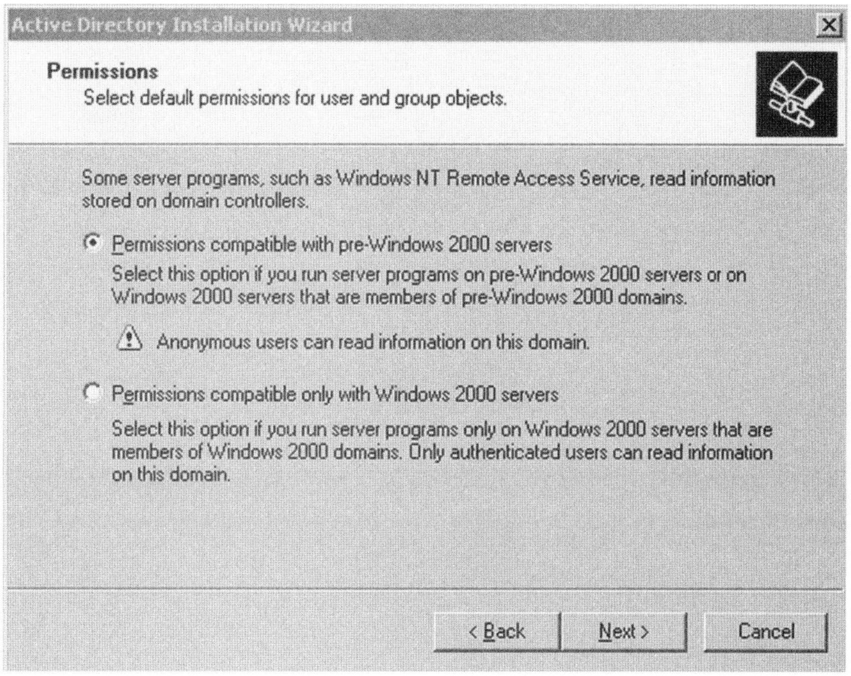

Figure 7.11 Unless you know for certain that there will only be Windows 2000 servers (or later) on your network, you should select permissions compatible with pre-Windows 2000 servers.

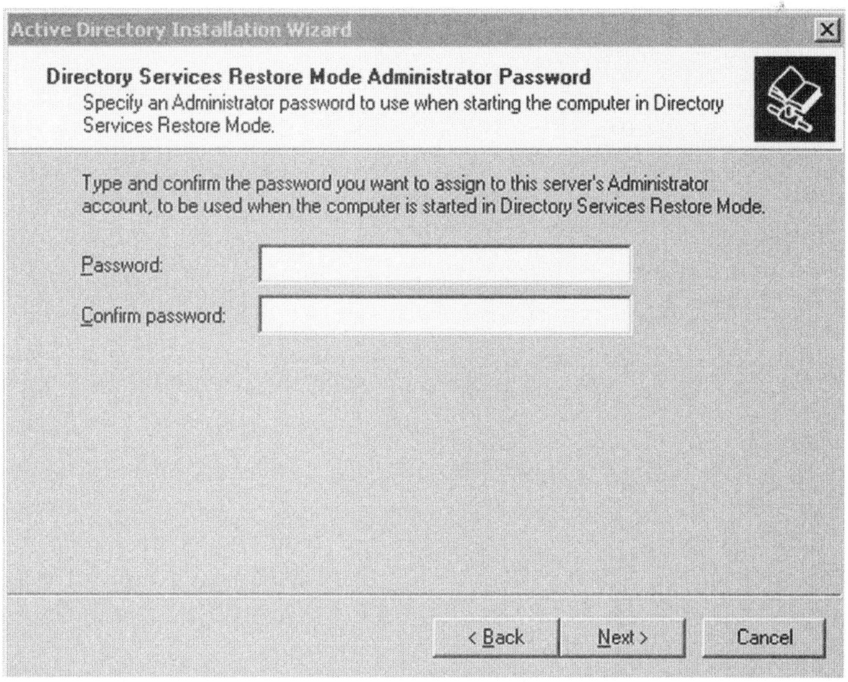

Figure 7.12 Establishing a password for Directory Services Restore Mode

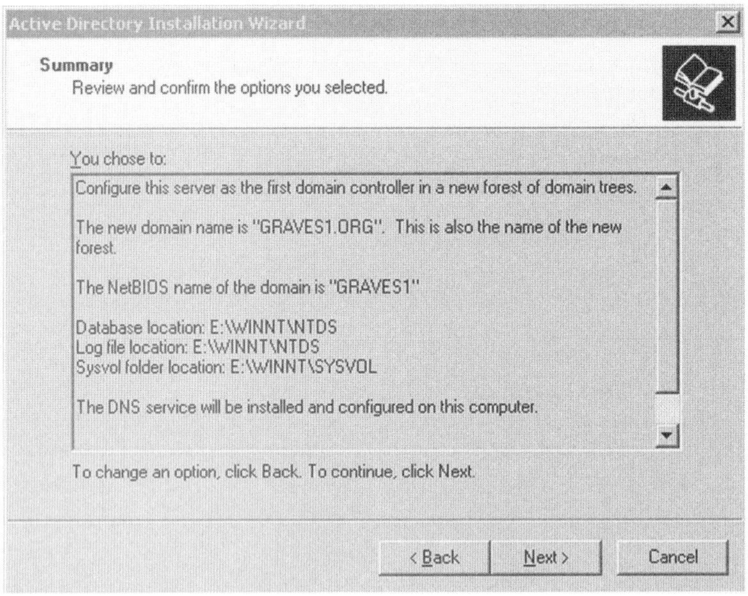

Figure 7.13 Confirming your DNS settings

Figure 7.14 Finishing the installation of DNS

12. This brings up the summary screen shown in **Figure 7.13** that simply confirms the data you entered. If anything that you see is incorrect, you have the opportunity to click the Back button until you get to the screen where that data was entered, and where you can make changes. If all is correct, click Next. The setup wizard will begin configuring Active Directory on your server. This can take a while, so now is a good time to review the steps you took to get to this point. Toward the end of this process you will be prompted to insert your W2KS CD into the drive and the Setup Wizard will copy some files from the CD.

13. Once the files are copied, a screen like the one in **Figure 7.14** will appear labeled Completing the Active Directory Installation Wizard. Click Finish.

Figure 7.15 Before your DNS configuration will have any effect, you must restart your server.

14. This brings up the screen shown in **Figure 7.15** informing you that your computer must be restarted for the changes to take effect. Click Restart Now and let your computer reboot.

EXERCISE 1 DISCUSSION

1. What is the purpose of running DCPROMO?

2. How does the Microsoft Active Directory relate to Novell's Directory Services?

3. If you're using servers on your network that have a NOS earlier than W2K, you need to configure your server to recognize permissions from these earlier machines. Why is this?

EXERCISE 2: CONFIGURING DHCP

You now have an effective domain controller for your W2K network. As it sits, however, you are going to have to statically assign an IP address to any client device you want to run on this network. In order to make life easier, you're going to make use of the Dynamic Host Configuration Protocol (DHCP) to automatically hand out IP addresses, as well as some other important information that I will discuss in this exercise. To complete the following exercises, you need only your newly configured domain controller.

EXERCISE 2A: STATICALLY ASSIGNING AN IP ADDRESS

For DHCP to properly run, DHCP Server must be running on a machine with a statically configured IP address. If you recall, during the installation of W2KS, you accepted the defaults. By default, your server is a DHCP client. Before you install DHCP you need to statically assign an IP to your server.

1. Right-click My Network Places on your desktop and select Properties. This will bring up a screen like the one in **Figure 7.16**.

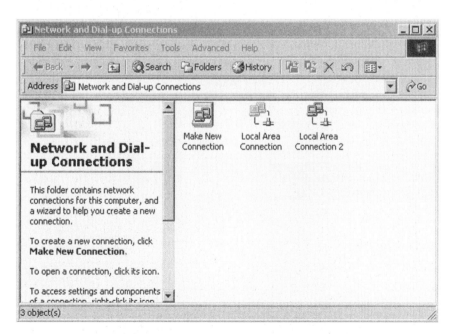

Figure 7.16 Configuring network settings in Windows 2000

(Note that in this illustration, there are two NICs installed. Do not be concerned with this.) Double-click Local Area Connection.

2. This brings up the Status window shown in **Figure 7.17**. Click Properties.

3. Under the General tab of the screen that appears, highlight Internet Protocol (TCP/IP) and click Properties. This will bring up the screen shown in **Figure 7.18**.

4. In your little network you will be using a Public IP address range. Assign the IP address of 192.168.0.100 to the machine named STUDENT1, 192.168.0.101 to STUDENT2, 192.168.0.103 to STUDENT3, and so on until all machines

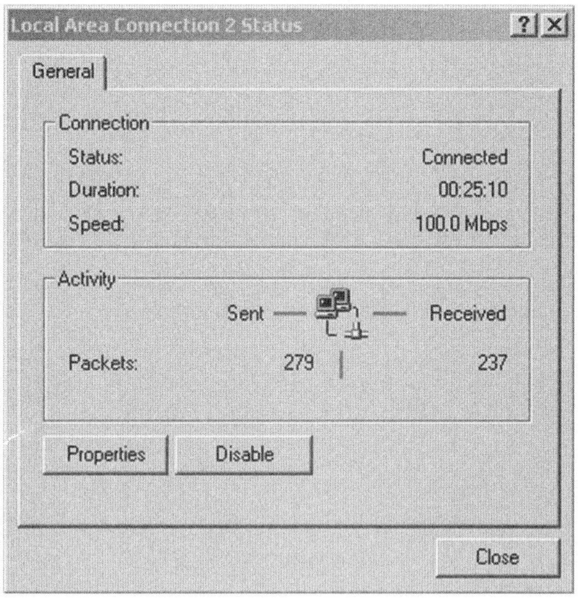

Figure 7.17   Status screen for network settings

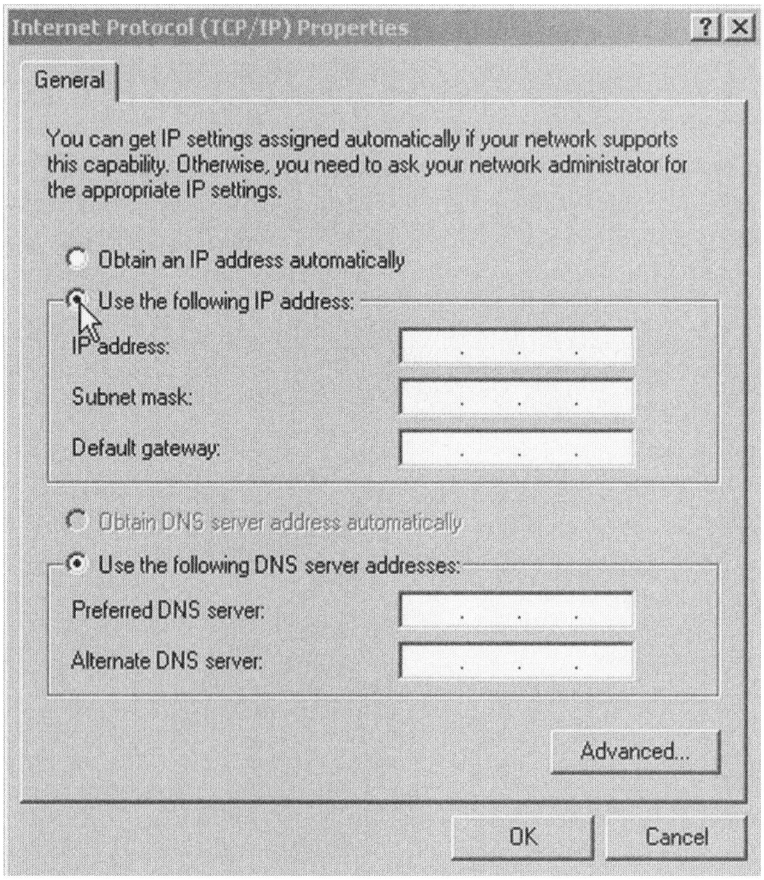

Figure 7.18   Configuring TCP/IP settings

have been assigned IP addresses. Record the total range of addresses used in this part of the exercise. Under the Subnet mask field, use 255.255.255.0 on all machines. Simply pressing <Tab> will fill in this value for you automatically.

5. When you click OK, you will be notified that since DNS is installed locally on that machine, the local IP address will be configured as the primary DNS server. Click OK. This brings you back to the Local Area Connection Properties screen. Click OK once again.

6. Close the Local Area Connection Status screen. It is not necessary to reboot the machine for the new configuration to take effect.

EXERCISE 2A DISCUSSION

1. If you are going to be using DHCP on your network, why does your server need to have a statically assigned IP address?

2. If this is your first server on the network, why doesn't Setup know to point to the local address for a DNS server?

EXERCISE 2B: INSTALLING DHCP

Now that you have a static IP configured on your servers, you can install and configure DHCP. This will enable your servers to dynamically configure DHCP clients on the network. You can also configure DHCP to automatically configure other values, such as default gateways and WINS servers. In the following exercise, you will configure DHCP.

1. Open Control Panel. You can do this either by double-clicking My Computer and then double-clicking the Control Panel icon in My Computer, or you can click Start>Settings>Control Panel.

2. Double-click Add/Remove Programs in the left-hand panel. This will bring up the screen shown in **Figure 7.19**.

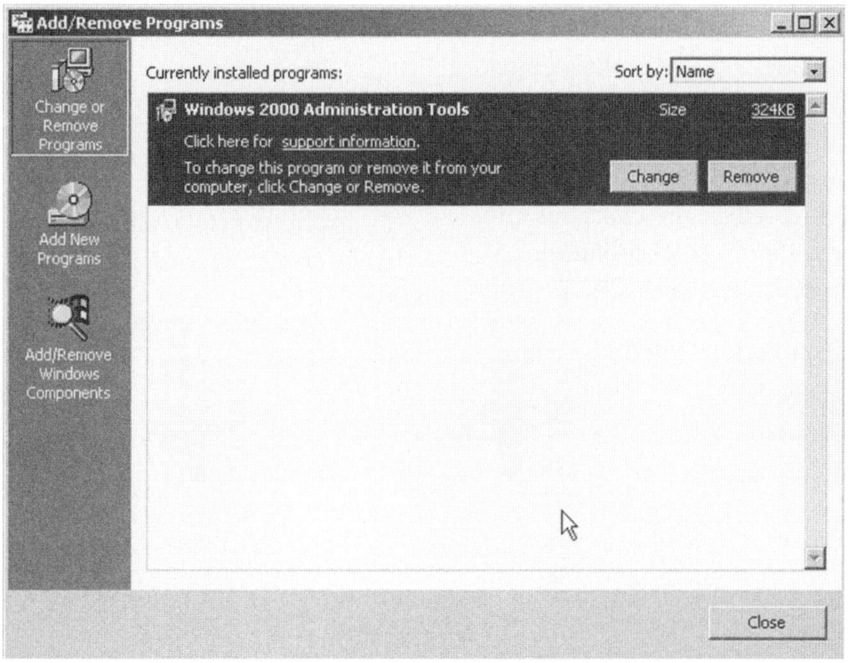

Figure 7.19 The Add/Remove Programs screen of Windows 2000

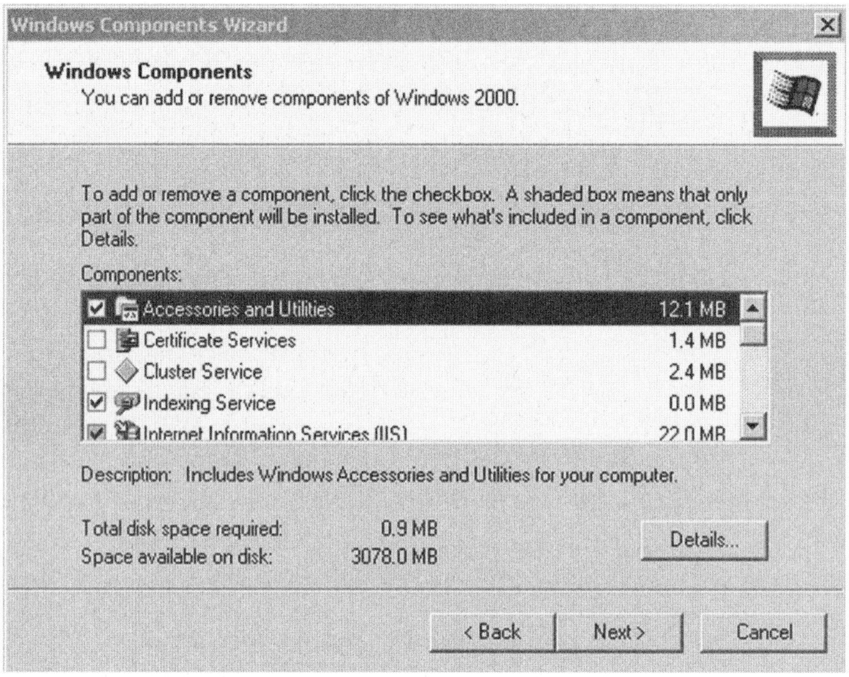

Figure 7.20 Changing Windows 2000 components

3. Click the Add/Remove Windows Components icon. This will bring up the screen shown in **Figure 7.20**.

4. In the Components window, scroll down until you see Networking Services. Highlight this selection and click the Details button. This brings a window like the one in **Figure 7.21**. Notice that DNS is already checked. Click the checkbox in front of Dynamic Host Configuration Protocol (DHCP) and click OK.

5. This brings you back to the Add/Remove Components window. Click Next and

your computer will start copying files. When it is finished copying files it will bring up the Completing the Windows Components Wizard screen shown in **Figure 7.22**. Click Finish and restart your computer.

EXERCISE 2B DISCUSSION

1. Why isn't DHCP installed by default as a network service?

2. From what screen do you add new network services to W2KS?

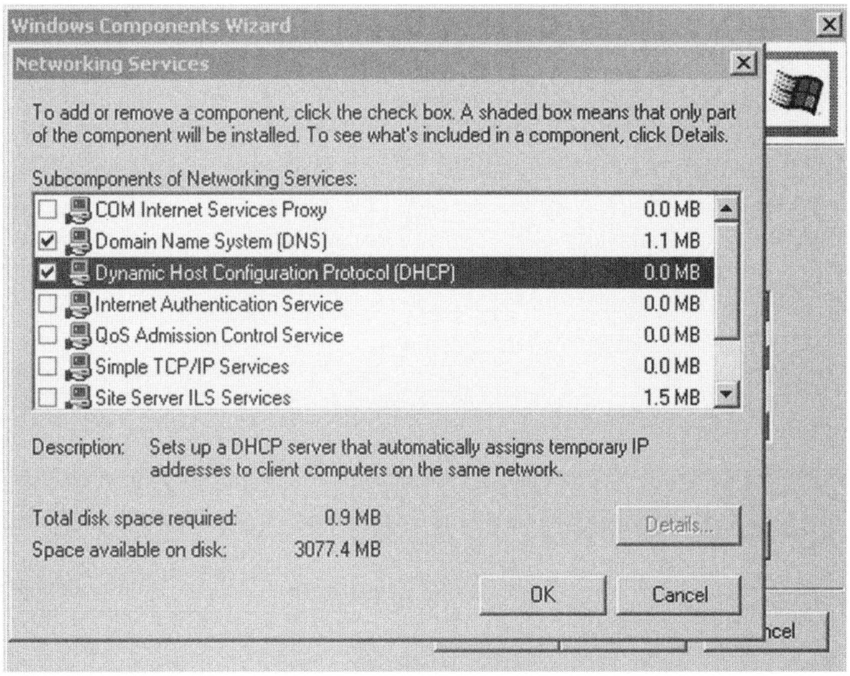

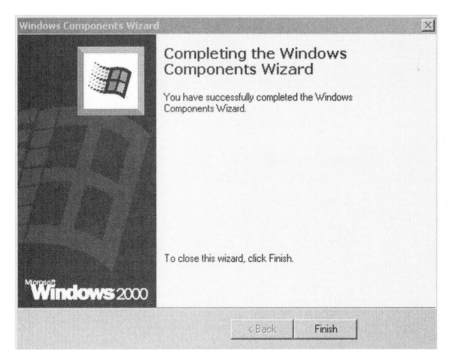

Figure 7.21   DHCP is found as a subcomponent of Networking Services.

Figure 7.22   Completing the Windows components installation

Exercise 2c: Configuring DHCP

Installing DHCP isn't enough. You now have to tell it everything it needs to know in order to function. If you click Start>Programs> Administrative Tools, you will find that you have a new menu item called DHCP (see **Figure 7.23**). Open this applet and get started.

1. Once the DHCP console is open, you'll have a screen like the one in **Figure 7.24**. As the screen tells you, the first thing you need to do is add a server.

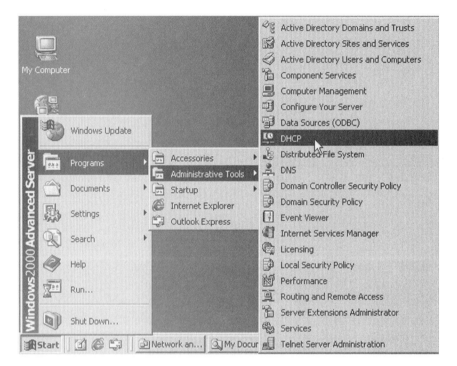

Figure 7.23   The DHCP Management Console is one of the Administrative Tools.

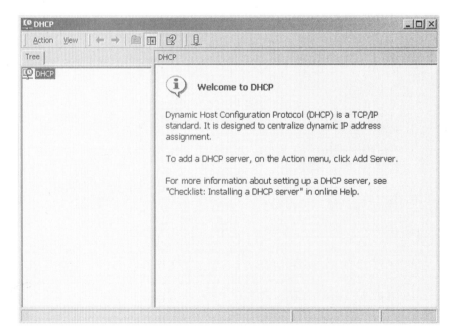

Figure 7.24   The DHCP Management Console

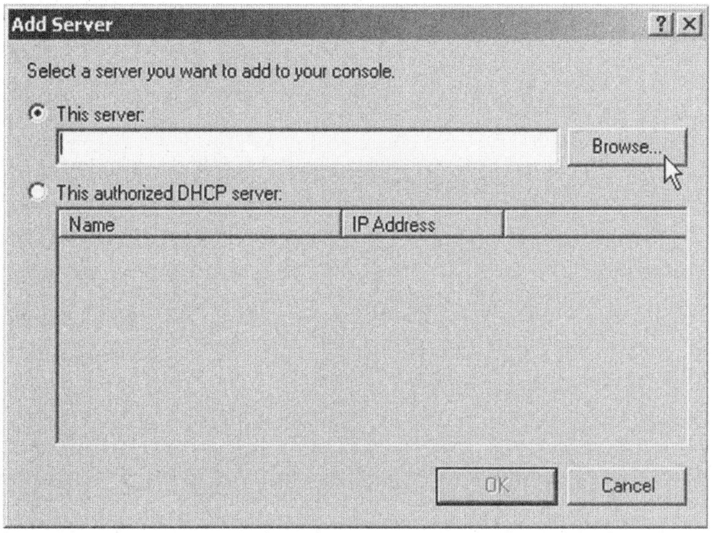

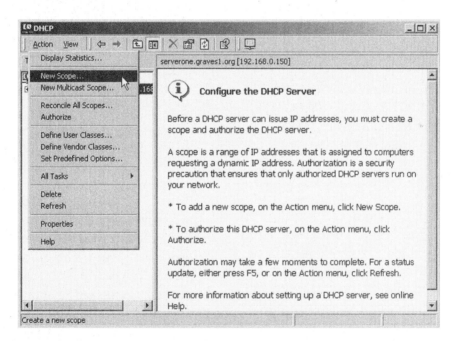

Figure 7.25 The first thing you need to do is add a server.

Figure 7.26 Next, you need to create a new scope.

2. Click the Action menu and select Add Server. The screen shown in **Figure 7.25** will appear. Click Browse and select your computer from the scroll-down list. (It should be the one listed.) Click OK.

3. Under the DHCP entry in the left-hand pane you should now see your server listed as a fully qualified domain name such as STUDENT1.STUDENT1.ORG. Highlight your server, and on the Action menu select New Scope (as shown in **Figure 7.26.**)

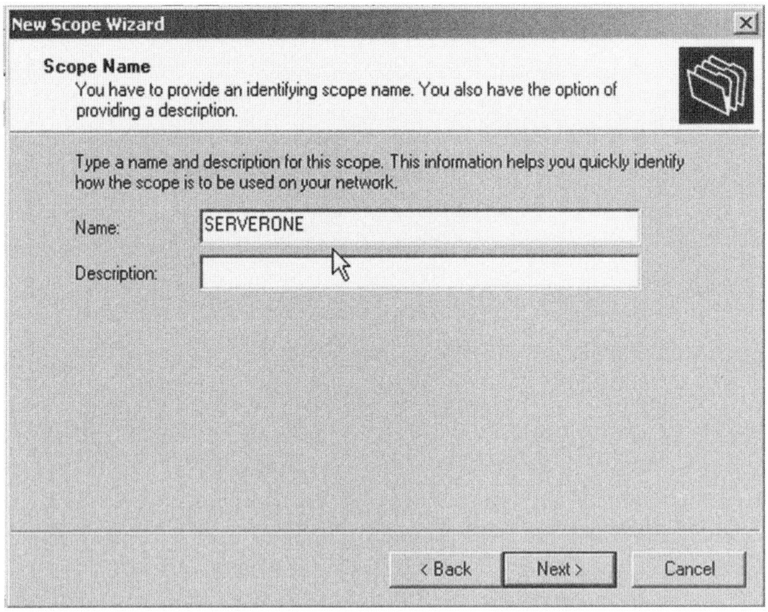

Figure 7.27 A single server can manage more than one scope, but each must have a unique name.

4. The first screen in the New Scope Wizard (**Figure 7.27**) prompts you to name the scope. You can use any naming convention you desire. For this class, give your scope the same name as your computer. The description is optional. Click Next.

5. The next screen prompts you to fill in your address range. Here you need to employ a little caution. If all of your servers have exactly the same range, then it is possible for more than one DHCP client to get the same address from different servers. Give each server a range of five IP addresses that will be unique on the network. Do not use any of the IP addresses from the range you used to statically configure the servers. Leave the Length and Subnet Mask fields alone and click Next.

6. The next screen (**Figure 7.28**) allows you to exclude a range of addresses from being handed out by DHCP. Here is where you would fill in the range of addresses you assigned to your servers. In a real world environment, you would want that range to be large enough to include not only your servers, but any IP printers and router interfaces you had on your network. Technically speaking, since you've assigned such a small range to each of your servers, and none of them includes the range of server addresses, you don't really need to fill in these values. So for now, leave the fields blank. Click Next.

7. The New Scope Wizard now allows us to specify how long a client may hang on to the address it was assigned. The default value is eight days (as shown in **Figure 7.29**). Accept this value and click Next.

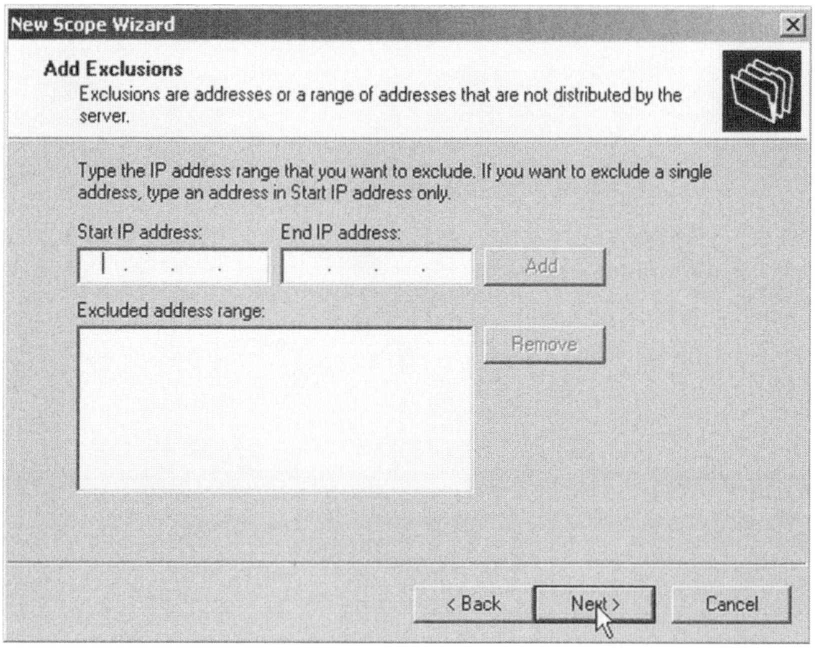

Figure 7.28 It is necessary to exclude any IP addresses on your network that have been statically assigned to any device.

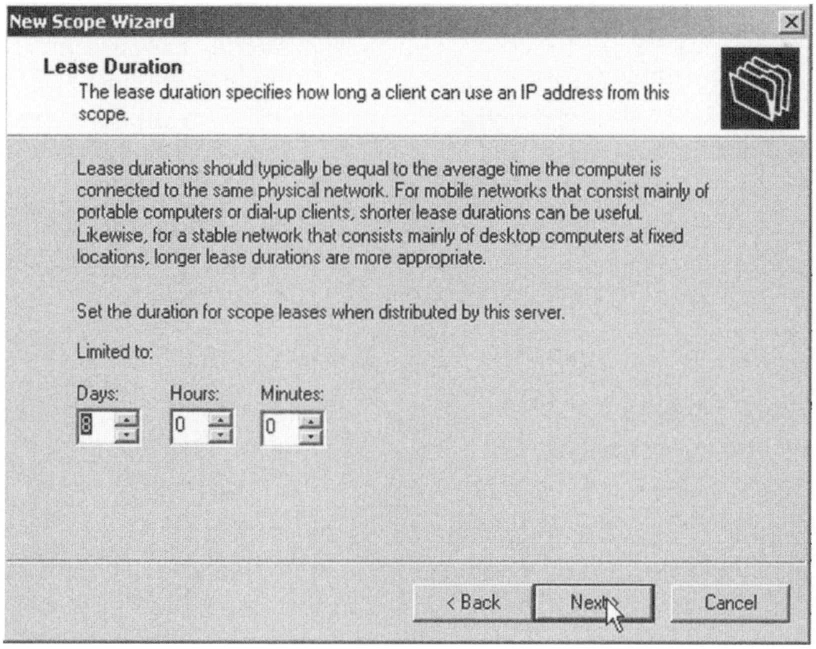

Figure 7.29 The lease specifies how long a client can hang onto the address it was assigned.

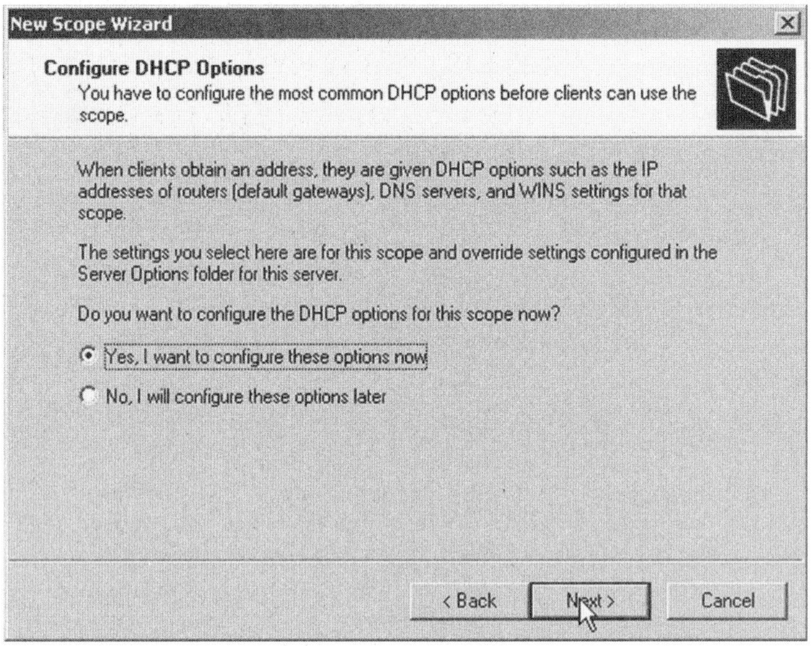

Figure 7.30 DHCP Options allows your server to configure clients with information other than just their IP addresses.

8. In the next screen (**Figure 7.30**), you are asked if you want to configure the DHCP options. Yes, you do, so make sure the option button Yes, I want to configure these options now is selected and click Next.

9. The next screens will include the following:

   • Router Configuration — Skip this screen.

   • Domain Name and DNS Servers — Fill in your domain name as configured during the Active Directory setup in the Parent Domain field. Put your server NetBIOS name in the Server Name field and click Resolve. That

should automatically fill in the IP address field for you. This screen is nearly identical to the one in the next step. (On a network with multiple DNS servers, you could add more by clicking Add and filling in the values for the additional servers.) Click Next.

   • WINS Servers — Fill in your NetBIOS name and click Resolve. Your screen should now look like the one in **Figure 7.31**. Click Next.

10. Now you are asked if you want to activate this scope (**Figure 7.32**). Click Yes, I want to activate this scope now, and then click Next.

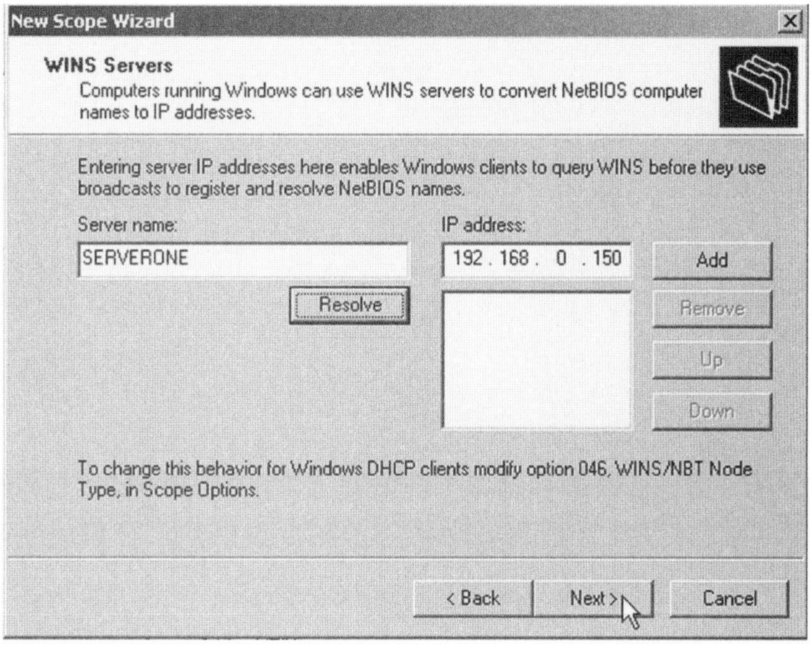

Figure 7.31 Configuring the WINS Server

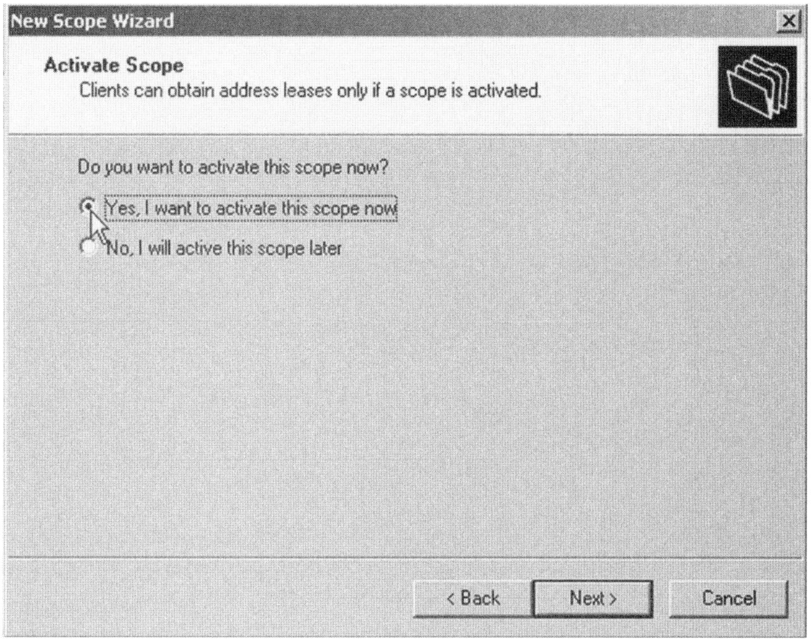

Figure 7.32 Before your newly configured scope can do anything, it must be activated.

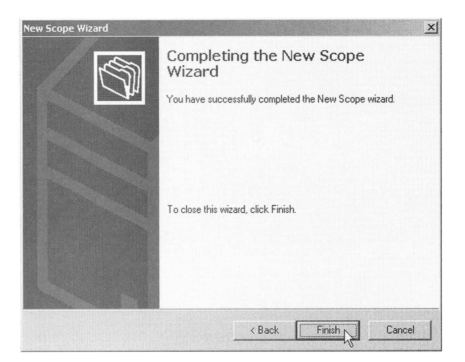

Figure 7.33 Completing the New Scope Wizard

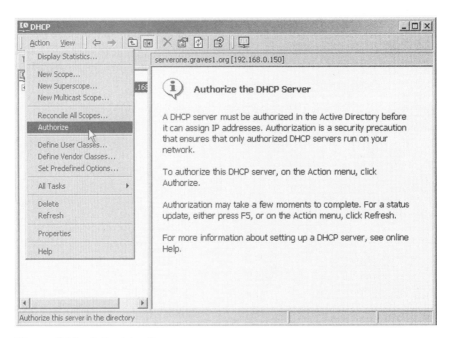

Figure 7.34 Authorizing the server

11. This brings up the Completing the New Scope Wizard screen shown in **Figure 7.33**. Click Finish.

12. Now, as the DHCP Console informs you, you must *authorize the server.* The configuration has been established, but until the server is authorized, it cannot hand out DHCP information. This prevents rogue DHCP servers from doling out unwanted information.

From the Action menu select Authorize (as shown in **Figure 7.34**). This may take a few minutes to finish. If nothing happens after a while, press <F5>. The scope should now appear underneath your server in the left-hand pane of the DHCP Console. DHCP has now been successfully installed and configured.

CHAPTER 2C DISCUSSION

1. What is a possible problem that could develop if you had two separate DHCP servers on the network configured with identical scopes?

2. You've just configured your server to act as a DHCP server. You've added the new scope, but none of your clients is getting IP information from the server. What are two possible reasons for this that are directly related to DHCP?

3. What are some of the optional settings you can configure in DHCP to assign to clients?

EXERCISE 3: ADDING A WORKSTATION TO THE DOMAIN

Now that you have a domain controller, you need something for it to control. After all, a king is nothing without his kingdom and a queen is nothing without her subjects. In this exercise, you will put your W2K Pro computers onto your newly created domains.

1. One of the machines from each team needs to be restarted. This time, when the menu appears asking which OS to start, select Windows 2000 Professional. Allow the computer to completely finish the restart before going onto the next step.

2. From the W2K Pro desktop, right-click My Computer and select Properties.

This will bring up the screen shown in **Figure 7.35**.

3. Click the Network Identification tab and click Properties. This will bring up the screen shown in **Figure 7.36**. Click the

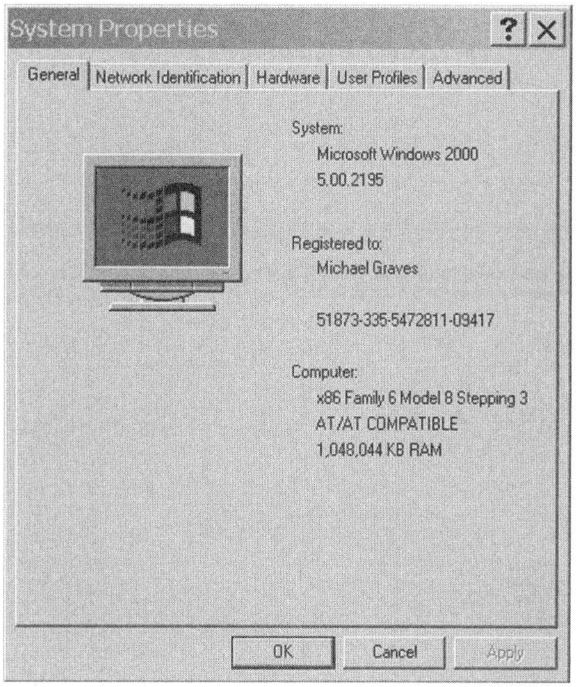

Figure 7.35 System Properties of a Windows 2000 machine

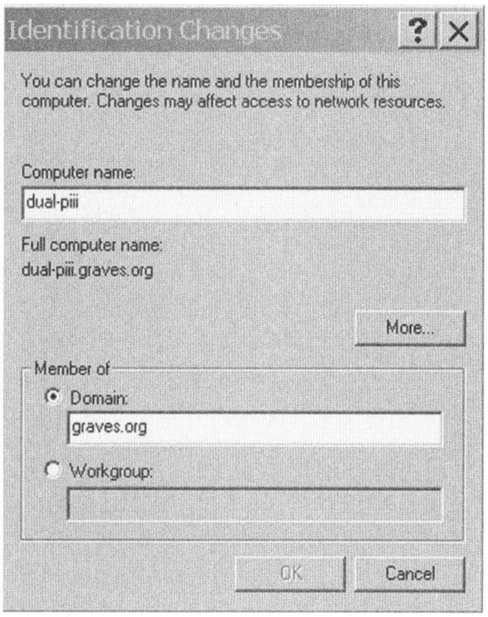

Figure 7.36 Adding a workstation to a domain

Domain option button and fill in the domain name assigned to your partner's computer (the one acting as the server). Click OK.

4. You will be prompted for a user ID and password for someone authorized to add this system to a domain. If everyone has been following instructions, you should be able to type `administrator` into the user ID field and `password` into the password field. It may take a while, but Windows 2000 should be able to successfully add this computer to the domain.

5. Restart both machines, reverse the roles of client and server, and repeat the above process.

WORKING WITH ACCOUNTS

INTRODUCTION

In the following exercises, you will be creating several different user and group accounts. These accounts will be used in later labs as you learn to associate permissions and apply security to individual users and groups. You will also learn to copy an account, so that its permissions and settings are automatically applied to the new account that you've created. In the final exercise, you will rename and finally disable the account.

MATERIALS

For these exercises, all you need is your machine, started as a domain controller.

NETWORK+ EXAM OBJECTIVES COVERED IN THIS LAB

3.1 Identify the basic capabilities (For example: client support, interoperability, authentication, file and print services, application support and security) of server operating systems to access network resources.

3.2 Identify the basic capabilities needed for client workstations to connect to and use network resources (For example: media,

network protocols and peer and server services).

3.4 Given a remote connectivity scenario comprised of a protocol, an authentication scheme, and physical connectivity; configure the connection.

EXERCISE 1: CREATING A NEW ACCOUNT

Any time a new user is added to the network, that person will require a unique user account. This account, complete with user ID and password, is the user's ticket to the network. In order to create the account, perform the following procedures.

1. Click on Start>Programs>Administrative Tools>Active Directory Users and Computers (as shown in **Figure 8.1**).

2. You should get a screen similar to that in **Figure 8.2**. Highlight Users in the left pane, then in the right pane, right-click in any blank area. From the pop-up menu that appears, select New>User.

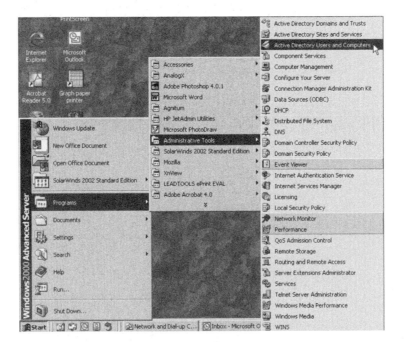

Figure 8.1 A road map to Active Directory Users and Computers

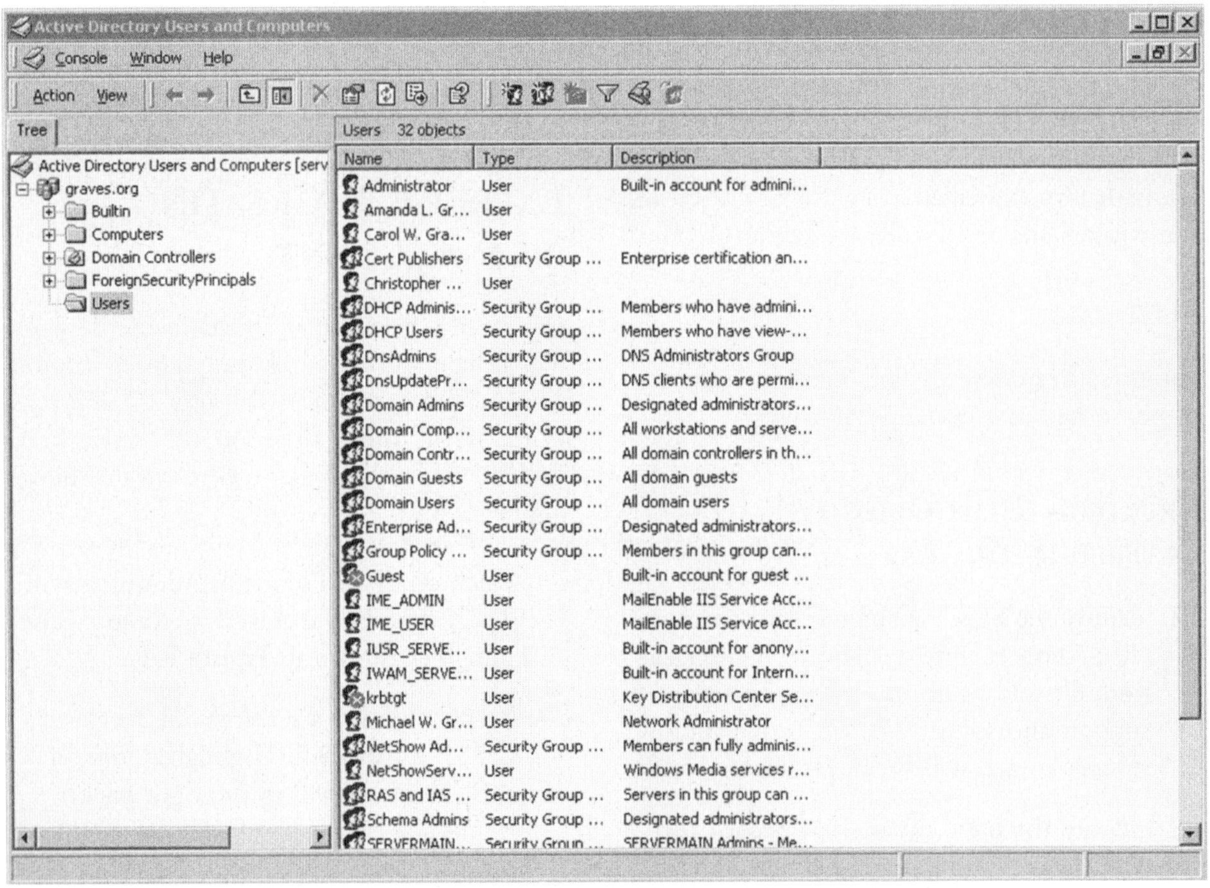

Figure 8.2 The Active Directory Users and Computers console

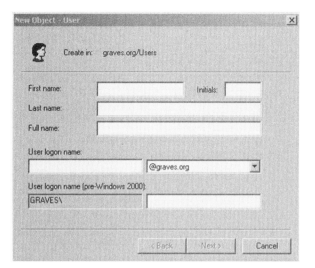

Figure 8.3 Fill in the user information and provide a unique User ID.

3. You should now have the dialog box shown in **Figure 8.3**. Type in the user information as requested. In the User Logon Name field, type in a User ID for the new user you are adding (you are just inventing users at this point). This must be a unique value. There can be no duplicate User IDs anywhere on the network. Click Next.

4. In the next dialog box (illustrated in **Figure 8.4**), you will be prompted to enter the user's password. You must enter it a second time in order to confirm the password. Should you inadvertently enter

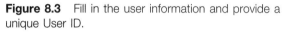

Figure 8.4 Next, enter a password, confirm it, and select the password options.

it differently the second time, the password will be rejected and you will have to start again. For all accounts in your lab exercises, you will be using *password* as the standard password. This will prevent forgotten passwords from becoming an issue. Obviously, in a real-world scenario, this would be a very bad idea. So type `password` into the Password and Confirm password fields.

5. There are four checkboxes beneath the password fields for password options. These options are as follows:

- User must change password at next logon — If this choice is selected, the first time users log onto their new accounts, they will be told that their passwords have expired and will be prompted to enter new ones (twice, for confirmation). This is the option to select if you want your users selecting their own passwords.

- User cannot change password — As the phrase implies, once you have assigned a password, it is etched in stone. Only an account administrator or someone with administrative privileges can change the password.

- Password never expires — If this field is selected, the password will remain valid until changed by an account administrator or someone with administrative privileges. This is the case even if the password policy has been set to force users to change their password periodically.

- Account is disabled — This option prevents anyone from logging onto the network using that particular account. It does not, however, delete any security settings or permissions for the account.

Select User cannot change password and click Next.

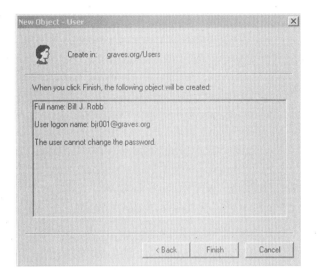

Figure 8.5 The User Summary screen

6. You will get a summary box like the one in **Figure 8.5**. All the information you typed in will be displayed except for the password. Click Finish. Your new account has been established.

7. Repeat the above steps until you have created a total of twelve new accounts. Don't forget to use *password* as the password for all user accounts.

EXERCISE 1 DISCUSSION

1. Which of the W2KS consoles did you use to create a new user account?

2. If you want your users to create their own passwords, what password option should you select when first creating their accounts?

3. What is a primary rule in creating a user ID for any given user?

EXERCISE 2: CREATING GROUP ACCOUNTS

Every network administrator quickly learns that managing multiple users all at once in groups of

MANAGING GROUPS

When you're first getting started with this networking business, it sometimes gets confusing when to use groups and when not to. And when it comes to managing groups, what's with this *global group* versus *local group*?

It isn't really all that complicated. Local groups are used to manage local resources. You might have a database containing your customer information. In order to allow access to that database, you create a local group called DATA. Permissions are assigned at this level.

Global groups are used to give users with similar sets of responsibilities and resource needs the permissions they need to do their work. For example, you might have a global group called SALES. Every salesperson needs access to the same resources and generally needs the same permission sets. Therefore, when you hire a new salesperson, rather than go through the rigmarole of assigning those permissions independently (and remembering what they are), you simply create a new account and add it to the SALES group. In order to give all sales reps access to the database, you add the global group SALES to the local group DATA. In one step, all sales reps were given exactly the same permissions to use the database.

A simple little mnemonic will help you remember what's going on. AGLP: *Accounts* go into *Global* groups, which are added to *Local* groups, which are given *Permissions*.

About the only time you *wouldn't* want to use global groups would be on a very small network with only a few users. In that case, it might actually be easier to manage the users individually. Even then, managing permissions on resources will be easier using local groups.

accounts is much simpler than trying to manage the users one at a time. In this section, you will create two forms of group accounts. You will create local groups to manage resources, and you will create global groups to manage users. Later on you will use these global groups to manage permissions.

EXERCISE 2A: CREATING A LOCAL GROUP

1. Start Active Directory Users and Computers, just as you did in Exercise 1. Right-click a blank portion of the right pane and select New>Group from the pop-up menu. You'll get the screen shown in **Figure 8.6**.

2. For Group Name, type in DOCUMENTS. Notice that the field labeled Group Name (pre-Windows 2000) is filled in for you. Beneath those fields, on the left are the options Domain local and Global. Select Domain local. For now, don't worry about group type. Click OK.

3. Repeat the process, creating a group called DATA.

EXERCISE 2B: CREATING A GLOBAL GROUP

1. Repeat the steps outlined in Exercise 2a. Name the group SALES. The one difference is that, instead of selecting Domain local in the second screen, select Global.

2. Repeat this process twice, creating global groups called MANAGEMENT and ADMINISTRATION.

EXERCISE 2 DISCUSSION

1. What was the key difference between creating a user account and creating a group account?

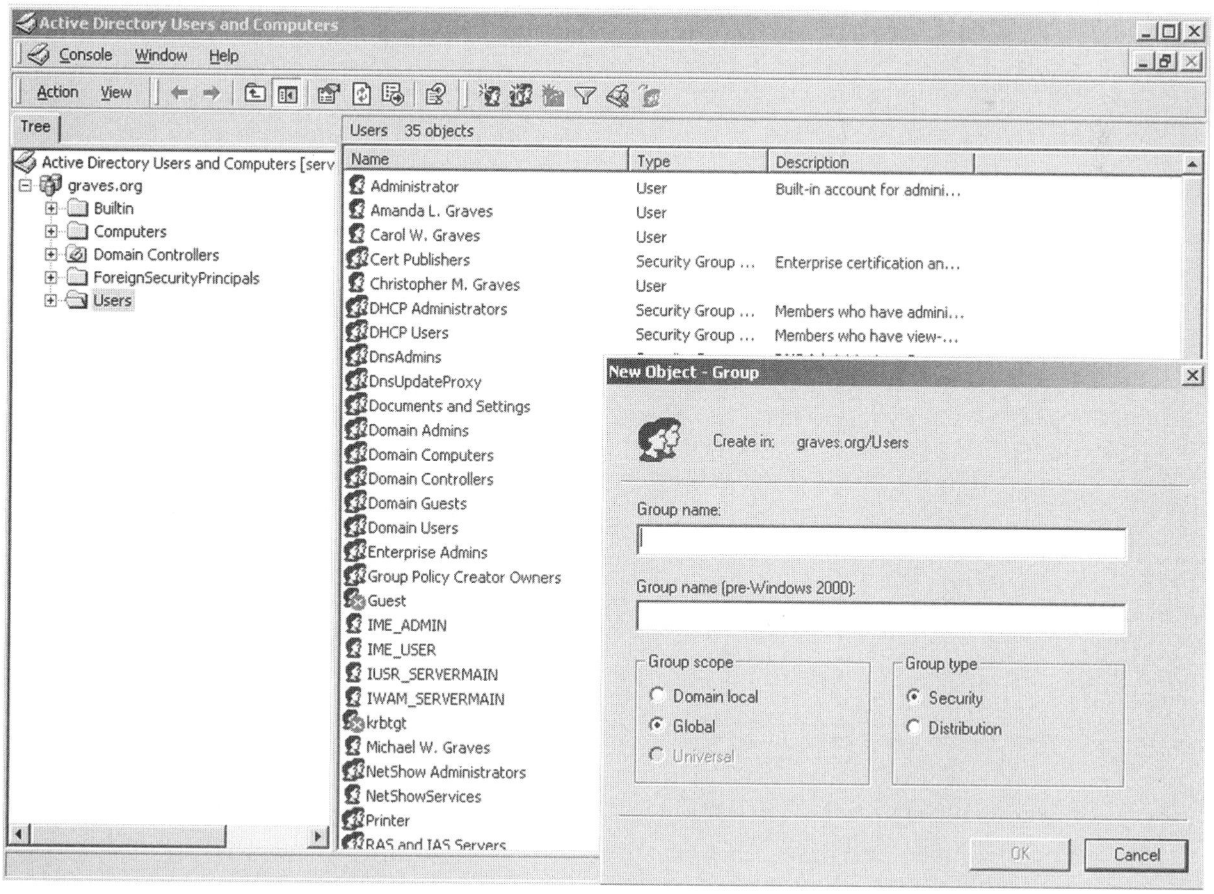

Figure 8.6   The New Group options in W2KS

2. What is the purpose of dealing with groups instead of handling each user on an individual basis?

EXERCISE 3: COPYING AN ACCOUNT

Now that you've created all those nearly identical groups and accounts the hard way, you will learn how you can take an account that has been configured the way you want and make a new one using the first one as a template.

1. The first thing you want to do is customize an account so that you know it is different from the others you created. Select one of the user accounts that you created in Exercise 1 and double-click it in the right pane of Active Directory Users and Computers. You'll get the dialog box shown in **Figure 8.7**.

2. Click the tab labeled Member Of. Then click Add. This will give you the screen

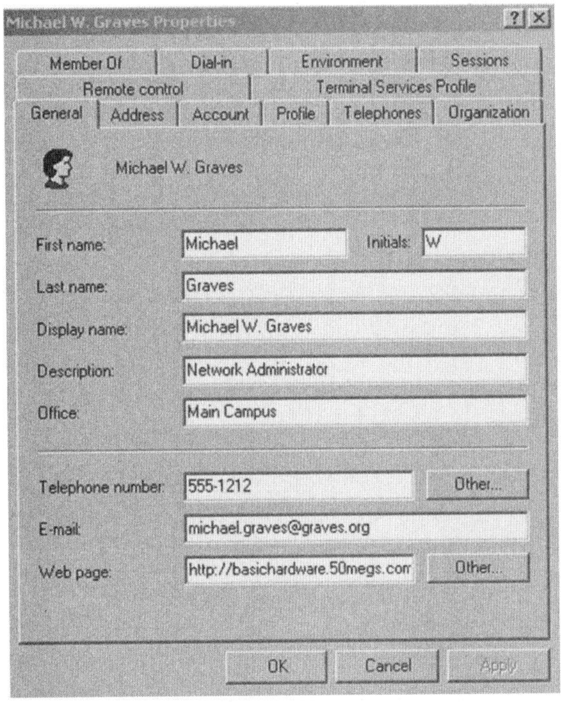

Figure 8.7 User Properties

shown in **Figure 8.8**. As shown in the illustration, add this account to the Backup Operators group and the Account Managers group. While you're at it, add it to your newly created SALES group. You can add multiple groups in one operation simply by holding down on the <Ctrl> key while you click on each group you wish to add. Click Add, then click OK.

3. Open the Users Folder in the left pane of Active Directory Users and Computers and right-click the account you just modified. Select Copy. Move on through the screens that follow. You'll notice that they are the same ones you saw when creating a new account. That is because that's exactly what you are doing, except this new account brings with it all the accoutrements of the account you copied.

EXERCISE 3 DISCUSSION

1. What purpose does copying an account serve when creating new accounts?

2. What aspect of a user account that you copy will apply to the new account you just created?

EXERCISE 4: RENAMING AN ACCOUNT

Once in a while it becomes necessary to rename an account. It's all too tempting to simply delete the old one and create a new one. However, there is a problem inherent in that procedure. It is not the user name, user ID, or password—or any combination of those things—that identifies the account to the OS. The account is identified by a 32-bit number that was generated by the OS when the account was created. This is the account's *security ID* (SID). If you want to keep the entire history of the account intact, you need

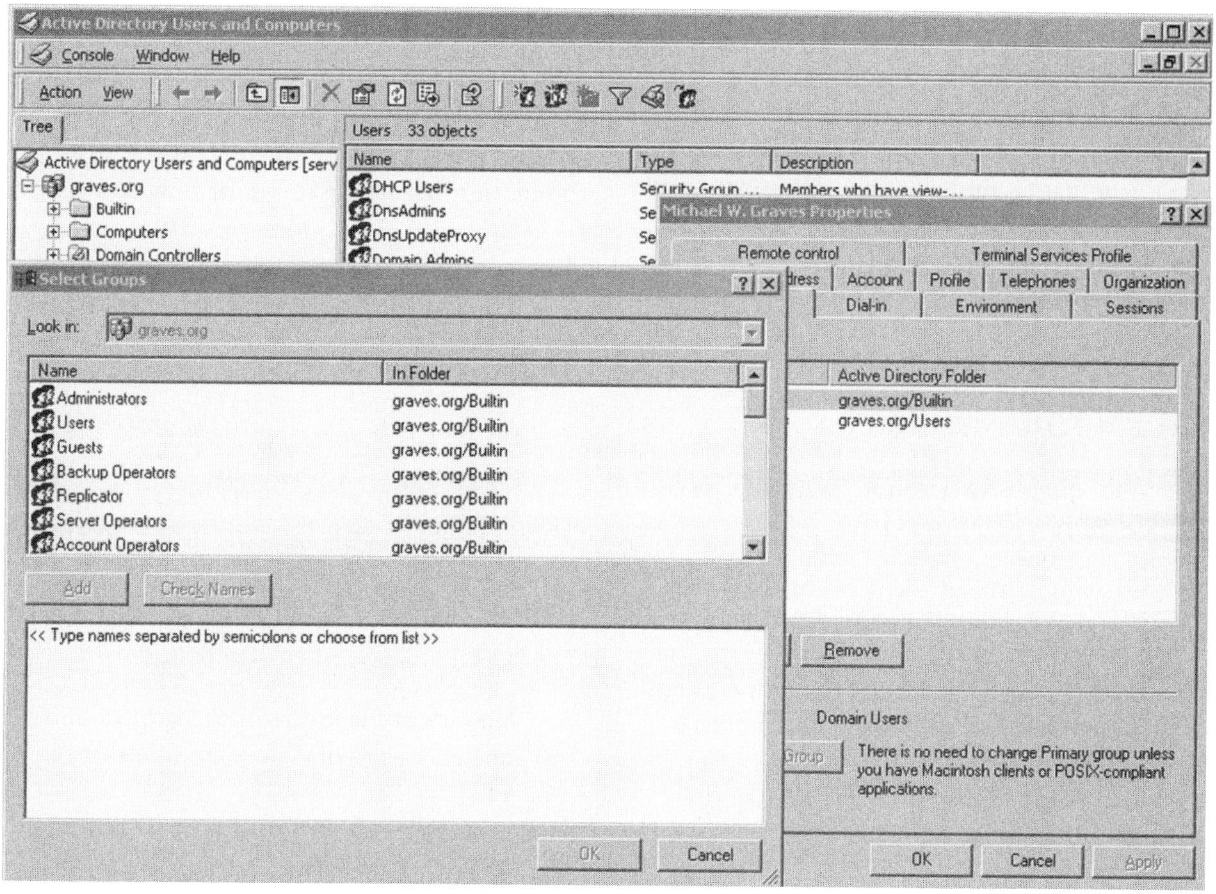

Figure 8.8 Joining a user account to a group account

to keep the SID intact. You do this by renaming the existing account. Here's how to do it.

1. Open Active Directory Users and Computers, and open the Users folder.

2. Right-click the account you want changed.

3. From the pop-up menu, select Rename.

4. Type in the new name for the account.

   It's as simple as that.

EXERCISE 4 DISCUSSION

1. Why rename an account? Why not just make a new one?

2. What property of the account makes it desirable to rename it rather than create a new one?

EXERCISE 5: DISABLING AN ACCOUNT

When a user leaves an organization, the first thing many administrators do is to delete that user's account. This can be (and frequently is) a critical error. The reason for not deleting a no-longer active account is the same as the one for not creating a new account for an existing user. That SID is the ticket to the account's history. Should you need to access that account for any reason, it won't be possible if the account and its SID were deleted. Simply re-creating the account won't work. Fortunately, disabling an account is one of the easiest things you'll ever have to do.

1. Open Active Directory Users and Computers, and open the Users folder.

2. Right-click the account you want disabled.

3. Select Disable.

Later on down the road, should you need to reactivate that account for any reason, you simply repeat the process. When you do that, the option Enable will have replaced Disable. Select Enable and the account will be reactivated.

Exercise 5 Discussion

1. Why disable an account? Why not just delete it?

2. What property of the account makes it desirable to disable rather than delete an account?

3. Can you set an account to be disabled automatically?

Exercise 6: Viewing Accounts

I will discuss Active Directory in detail in Lab Nine, but here is a glimpse of how it is useful.

1. Open Active Directory Users and Computers. To do this, click Start>Programs> Administrative Tools>Active Directory Users and Computers.

2. In the left-hand pane, right-click one of the users you created, and from the menu select Properties. Spend a few minutes opening each of the tabs in the window that appears and filling in the information. Be creative. This is your chance to be just like Stephen King.

3. Now right-click one of the groups you created earlier and do the same thing.

SECURING ACCOUNTS AND RESOURCES

INTRODUCTION

One of the chief reasons for setting up a network to begin with is to provide the ability to share data and other resources. Unfortunately, this goal is at odds with one of your other major objectives, which is to keep your network secure. Good network operating systems provide the means for doing both.

Accounts or resources can be either allowed or blocked from specific users or groups by setting permissions. In the past, there have been different ways of securing resources. Microsoft products have historically provided the network administrator with the ability to use either *share-level* or *user-level* security. Most advanced NOSs also offer *file system security*. NTFS permissions are an example of file system security.

In the following exercises, you will be looking at ways to implement user-level security and at how to apply NTFS permissions to an account. Microsoft's Windows 2000 (and later) OS also have something called Active Directory. While it is far beyond the scope of this course to provide detailed instruction in managing Active Directory, I do feel that an overview is essential. Therefore, I will take you through a brief look at Active Directory.

MATERIALS

- The computers on which the students installed W2KS in the previous lab

- A good attention span

NETWORK+ EXAM OBJECTIVES COVERED IN THIS LAB

3.1 Identify the basic capabilities (For example: client support, interoperability, authentication, file and print services, application support and security) of server operating systems to access network resources.

3.2 Identify the basic capabilities needed for client workstations to connect to and use network resources (For example: media, network protocols and peer and server services).

4.4 Given a troubleshooting scenario involving a client accessing remote network services, identify the cause of the problem (For example: file services, print services, authentication failure, protocol configuration, physical connectivity and SOHO (Small Office/Home Office) router).

4.5 Given a troubleshooting scenario between a client and server environments, identify the cause of a stated problem.

EXERCISE 1: MANAGING PERMISSIONS

The most rudimentary security of any NOS is the ability to enforce specific permissions onto groups and/or individual accounts. In the following two exercises you will first apply permissions to an account. Then you'll take a look at the effect those permissions have on the ability of that user to perform certain tasks.

EXERCISE 1A: SETTING UP USER-LEVEL PERMISSIONS

For this lab, you are going to start the student machines as Windows 2000 Servers. User-level permissions are the most basic permissions you can apply to a resource. They are applied at the resource level, but rely on users' credentials to determine what level of access a particular user will be given. Any user who creates a folder can apply user-level permissions to that folder. To do this, simply follow these steps.

1. The first thing you need to do is share the directory. To do that, open Windows Explorer by right-clicking Start and selecting Explore. By default, this method will bring you to the Start Menu subdirectory within the directory of the user who is logged on. This is located in the Documents and Settings directory.

2. In Lab Four, you created individual directories that were identified with your first names. Browse to that folder, right-click it, and select Sharing (as shown in **Figure 9.1**).

3. This will bring up the screen shown in **Figure 9.2**. Note the options on this screen. For one thing, you can rename

the share to something other than your directory name. Do note, however, that certain characters that are permitted in file names in NTFS or FAT32 file systems are not permitted as network shares. You can also limit the number of users you allow to access this resource at the same time. For now, just click the button labeled Permissions.

4. This will bring up the screen shown in **Figure 9.3**. In the upper portion of that screen is a window labeled Name. This is where you add the users that you want to allow access to this folder. Below are three different permission levels. These permissions can be either allowed or denied. Denying permission prevents users from exercising that permission regardless of any other privileges they may have. For instance, denying Read permission prevents a user from even opening a folder. The three permissions are:

- Full Control — This allows users to do anything they want with that folder. They can add, delete, or edit this resource or anything contained within to their hearts' content. They can also change permissions or take ownership of that folder.

- Change — Users with Change privileges can add to the folder, delete items from the folder, or edit its contents. They cannot, however, change permissions or take ownership.

- Read — Users with Read permissions can access the data contained within the folder, but they cannot change it in any way. A file with Read permissions that is altered may only be saved under a different file name. If the folder itself has only Read permissions applied, then the file must not only be renamed, it must be saved to a different folder.

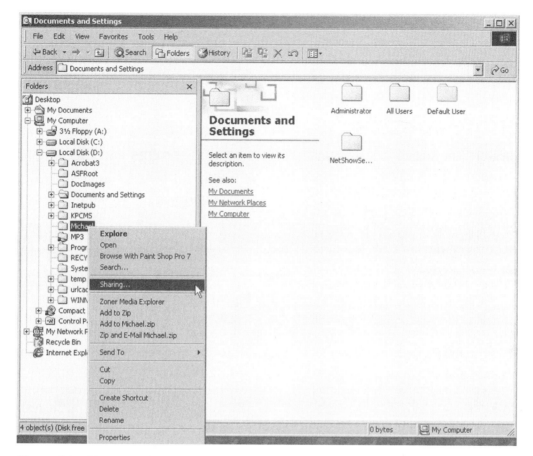

Figure 9.1   Sharing a folder in Windows Explorer

Figure 9.2   Sharing options in Windows 2000

Figure 9.3   User-level permissions in Windows 2000

5. Clicking Add next to the Name window will bring up a window entitled Select Users, Computers, or Groups (as shown in **Figure 9.4**). For now, leave the group intact, but in the real world, if you want your network to even closely resemble a secure network, you'll want to highlight the default group called Everyone and click Remove. Browse down the listing in the upper pane and select three of the users you created in Lab Eight. In order to select multiple users, hold down on the <Ctrl> key and click the accounts you've chosen. Click Add to add them to this folder. Now, in the permissions box, click only the Read box and make sure all others are deselected. Click OK.

6. You're back to the previous screen. Notice now that if you highlight the Everyone group, all three boxes are checked. This is why you want to remove that group. The users you added are to have Read permissions only. The users you've added are automatically members of the Everyone group. Click Apply.

7. Click Add once again and add three more users from those you created. This time give them Change permissions. Click Apply and then OK.

EXERCISE 1A DISCUSSION

1. With user-level permissions, can two different users be assigned different permissions?

2. Can users with Read permissions change a file? If so, can they save that file?

EXERCISE 1B: PERMISSIONS AT WORK

Now take a look at what you accomplished by setting those permissions. The first thing you will need to do is to restart some of your machines. One person on each team should keep his or her machine running as a server, while the other restarts his or her machine to Windows 2000 Professional. On the latter machine, log on as one of the users that was

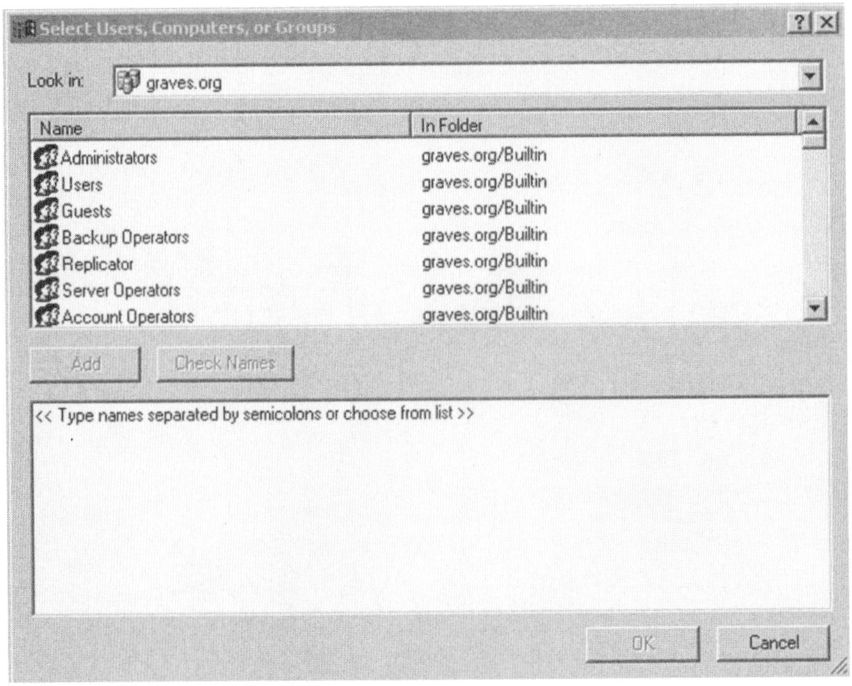

Figure 9.4 Adding a user or group to the permissions list

given Read permissions to the resource used in Exercise 1a.

1. The document that you created in Lab Four should still be present in the folder. Open that document and add a couple of paragraphs of text to the end.

2. Try to save the document. What happened?

3. Now select File>Save As, and browse to the My Documents directory and give it a new name. Now what happens?

4. Click Start>Shut Down, and on the scroll bar scroll down to Log Off [your user name]. Log on as one of the users that was assigned Change permissions.

5. Repeat steps 1 and 2 and log your results. This time you should have been successful at saving the file.

EXERCISE 1B DISCUSSION

1. What steps do users with Read permissions have to take in order to save files they're altered?

2. Do Read permissions apply to a directory or a file?

EXERCISE 2: SETTING NTFS PERMISSIONS

Users of the NTFS file system have the ability to apply security to their resources that is enforced by the file system itself. These are known as *NTFS permissions*. In this exercise I will demonstrate how much more granular and flexible security can be when NTFS permissions are used instead of user-level permissions.

1. Start by creating or moving several files into the folder you created using your own first name. For the purposes of this lab, I have moved several screen shots

into my folder. You should browse to the WINNT directory and, using the <Ctrl> button, select all the files with a .bmp extension. Right-click these files after they are selected and select Copy from the menu that appears. Go back to the directory you created in the left pane of Explorer, right-click and select Paste. Do not simply drag the files from one location to the other!

2. In Windows Explorer, right-click one of the files within your folder and select Properties. This will bring up the screen shown in **Figure 9.5**.

3. Clicking the Security tab will bring up a screen similar to that shown in **Figure 9.6**. Notice first of all that you have some additional options you didn't have in simple user-level security. In addition to Full Control and Read permissions, you also have:

   • Modify — This is similar to the Change permission in user-level security.

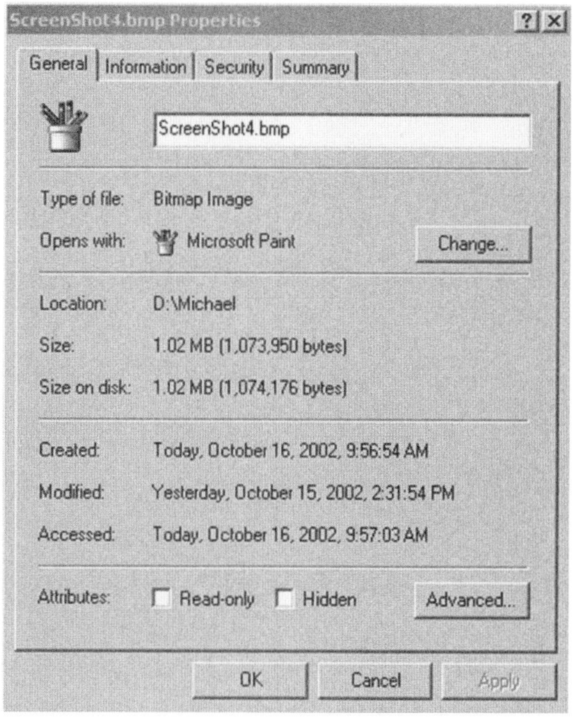

Figure 9.5 File Properties in Windows 2000

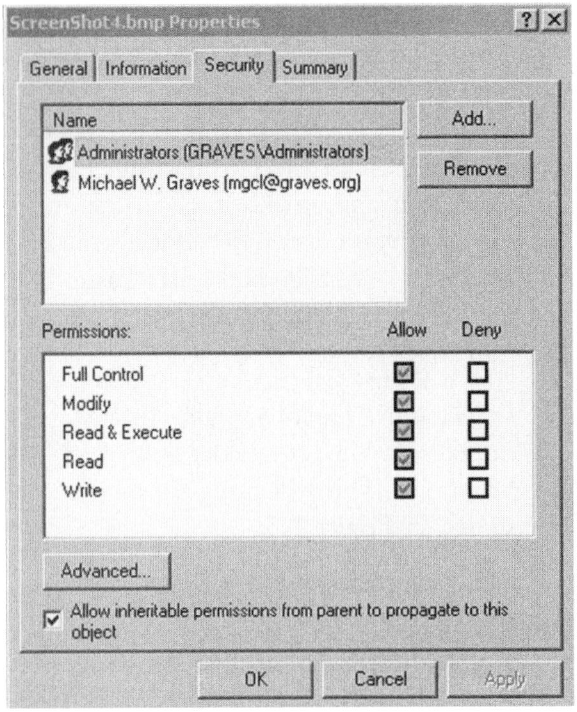

Figure 9.6 Basic NTFS permissions

- Read and Execute — In addition to being able to read files in the folder, a user can run executable programs. Read permission alone will not allow execution of programs.

- Write — Users with only Write permission can add files to the folder, but they cannot access and/or modify existing files contained within it.

4. Now click the Add button next to the Name window. This will bring up the screen shown in **Figure 9.7**. Here is where you can add users and groups to the list of people who have access to this resource.

5. Scroll down until you find the SALES group that you created in Lab Eight. To add the group you can either double-click

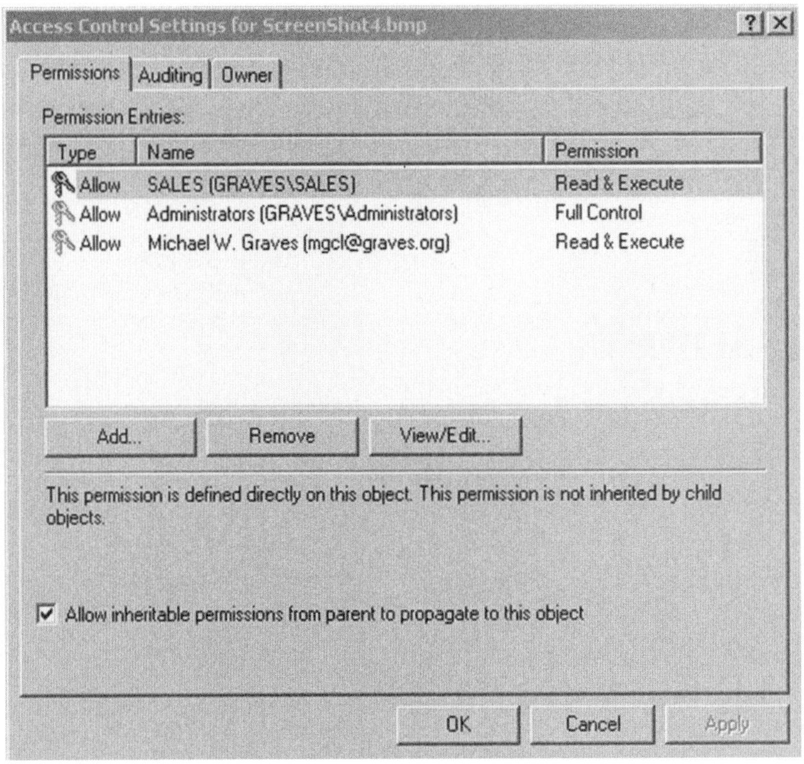

Figure 9.7 Adding a user or group to NTFS permissions

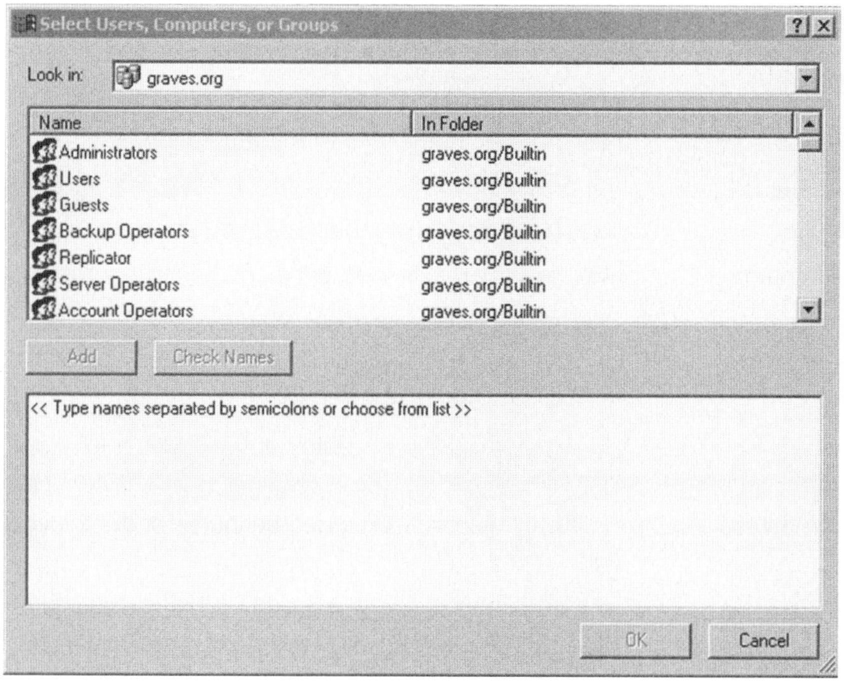

Figure 9.8 Editing permissions for a user or group

that group or highlight the group and click Add, and then OK.

6. This brings you back to the previous screen, but now the SALES group has been added to the Name window. Notice that the only permissions currently assigned to that group are Read & Execute and Read.

7. Now click the Advanced button beneath the Permissions window. This will bring up a window like the one in **Figure 9.8**. Highlight SALES and click View/Edit.

The window that appears (see **Figure 9.9**) allows you to set the NTFS Access Permissions. As you can see, these permissions allow much more control over access to a given resource. **Table 9.1** gives a brief description of each permission.

9. For the SALES group, click the Create Files/Write Data and the Create Folders/Append Data. Click OK on

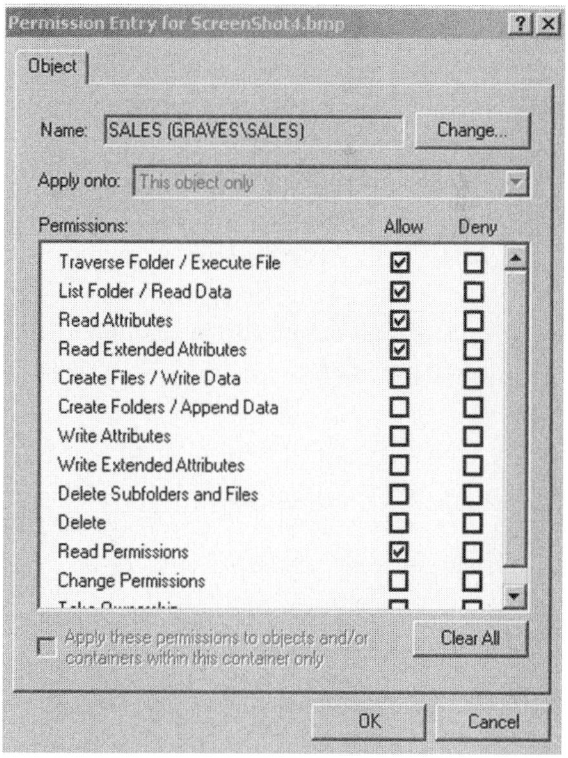

Figure 9.9 Advanced NTFS permissions

NTFS Access Permissions

Permission Name	Permission Function
Traverse Folder/Execute File	User may browse folder and/or execute programs
List Folder/Read Data	User may view the contents of the folder and open files
Read Attributes	User may view the attributes of a file or folder
Read Extended Attributes	User may view extended attributes of a file or folder
Create Files/Write Data	User may create a new file
Create Folders/Append Data	User may create subdirectories within the folder and/or edit the contents of files contained within it
Write Attributes	User may reset the attributes of the folder or any files contained within it
Write Extended Attributes	User may reset the extended attributes of the folder or any files contained within it
Delete Subfolders and Files	User may remove subdirectories or their contents from the folder
Delete	User may delete anything from the folder or even the folder itself
Read Permissions	User may view the permissions applied to the folder, including those of other users
Change Permissions	User may alter the permissions assigned to the folder and its contents
Take Ownership	User may assume ownership of the file or folder (inherently giving Full Control over the resource)

each screen until you are back to the Windows Explorer screen. You have now set NTFS permissions on a file. Now any user you add to the SALES group will automatically be assigned those permissions.

EXERCISE 2 DISCUSSION

1. What are some of the advantages of NTFS permissions over User-Level permissions?

2. You've just had a user create a new database file for company use that contains a great deal of sensitive information. What step should you, as an administrator, take to further protect that data?

3. In what significant way does Change permission differ from Full permission?

EXERCISE 3: AN OVERVIEW OF ACTIVE DIRECTORY

Windows 2000 Server products introduced the concept of directory services to their software in the form of Active Directory. Active Directory treats each resource on the network, whether it be a file or folder on a hard drive, a printer, or a user, as if it were a file or folder on a hard drive. This allows for more precise and centralized administration of the network.

Virtually any change you make to the network alters the contents of Active Directory. Adding a new server, adding new users, or adding a new printer are all things that register changes. However, Microsoft has made it easy to access and manage Active Directory through three consoles. These consoles are accessed by clicking Start>Programs>Administrative Tools. They are Active Directory Domains and Trusts, Active Directory Sites and Services, and Active Directory

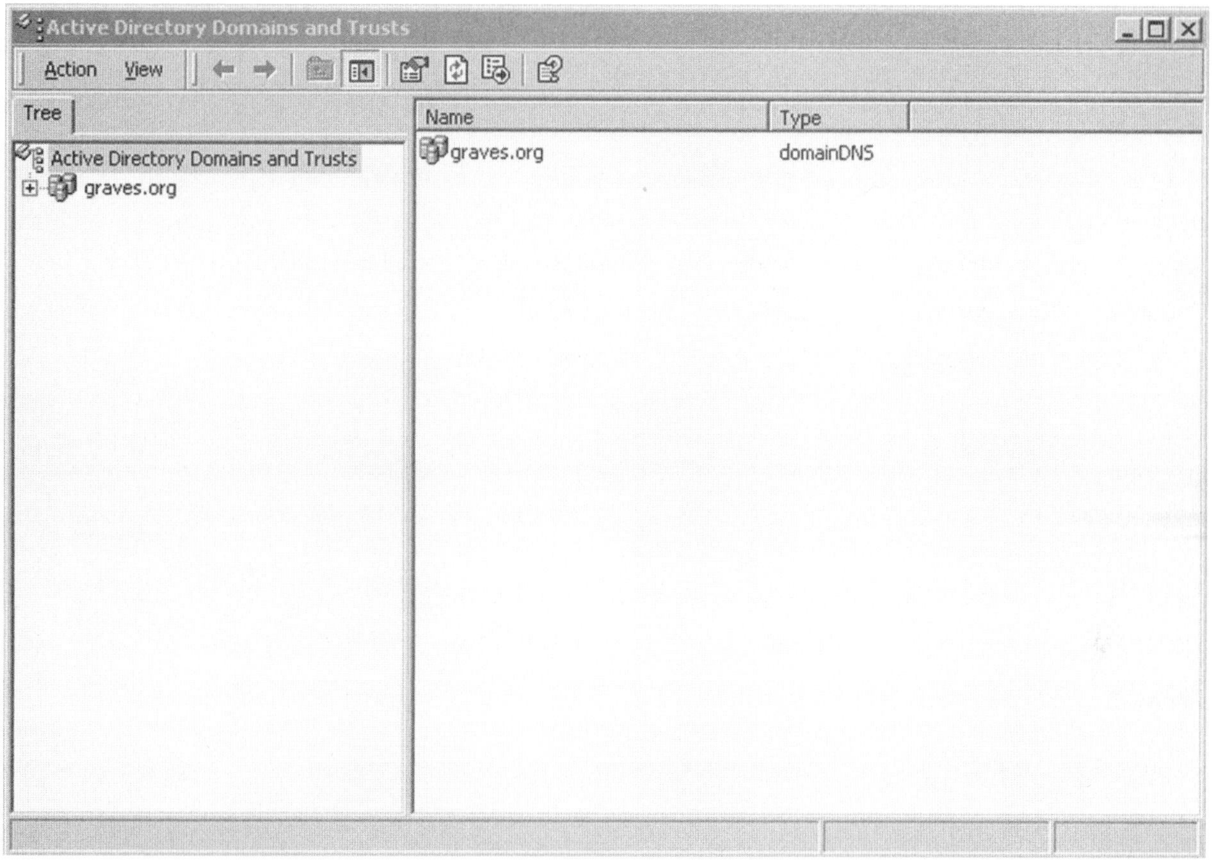

Figure 9.10 Active Directory Domains and Trusts

Users and Computers. A complete overview of Active Directory is the subject of an entire course. Since it is not the purpose of this particular course to provide instruction in Microsoft operating systems, I will limit this section to a very brief tour of what each console does.

EXERCISE 3A: ACTIVE DIRECTORY DOMAINS AND TRUSTS

1. Click Start>Programs>Administrative Tools>Active Directory Domains and Trusts. This will bring up the screen shown in **Figure 9.10**.

2. Right-click your domain name and select Properties. This will bring up the screen in **Figure 9.11**. The General tab tells you the pre-Windows 2000 domain name and in what mode the domain currently

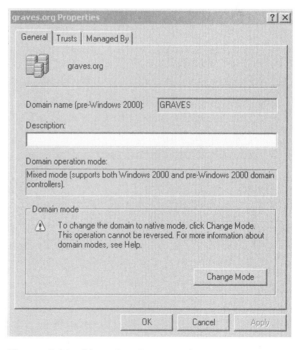

Figure 9.11 Managing the properties of a domain

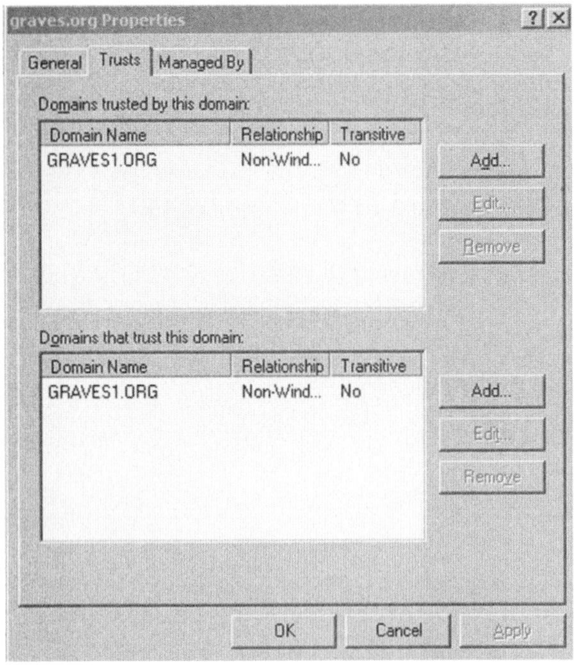

Figure 9.12 Creating trusts between domains

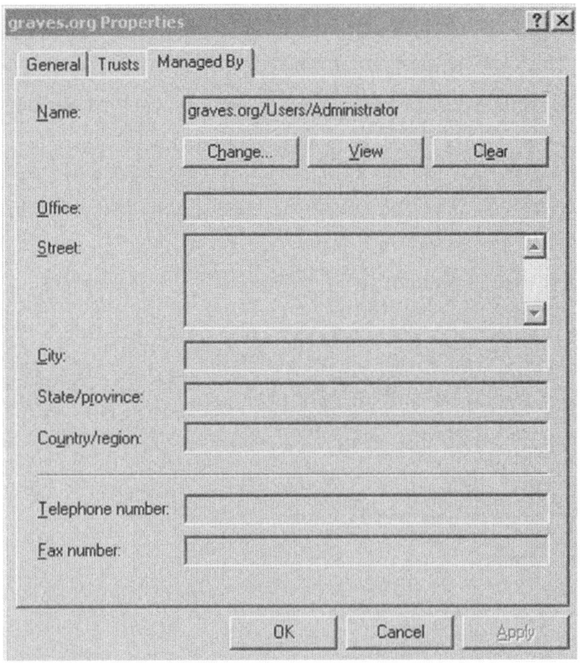

Figure 9.13 Viewing data for the managing administrator

operates. Mixed mode means that permissions from pre-Windows 2000 servers are being supported. Native mode means that only Windows 2000 permissions are supported. The Change Mode button allows you to change from Mixed mode to Native mode one time only. It is not a reversible change.

3. Clicking the Trusts tab brings up the screen shown in **Figure 9.12**. Here is where trusts between domains are created. Note in this illustration that I have created a trust with another domain on my network.

4. Click the Managed By tab and you will get the screen in **Figure 9.13**. Note that in this example there is no data filled in for the Administrator. Maybe you should correct that oversight.

5. Click the View button to get the screen shown in **Figure 9.14**. This will bring up the Administrator Properties. Fill in the

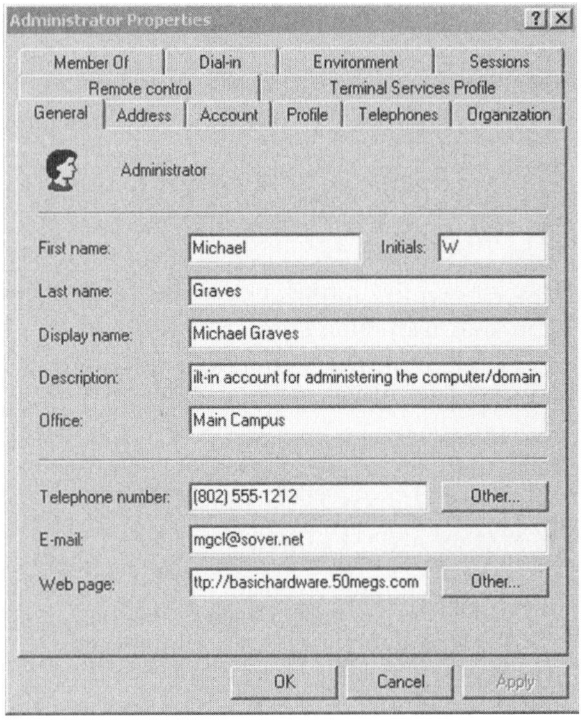

Figure 9.14 Editing data for the managing administrator

information in the General tab and in the Address tab. Click Apply and then OK. On the next screen click OK. This will bring you back to Active Directory Domains and Trusts once more. Now when you open the Properties window and select Managed By, all that information is available.

EXERCISE 3B: ACTIVE DIRECTORY SITES AND SERVICES

1. Click Start>Programs>Administrative Tools>Active Directory Sites and Services. This will bring up the screen shown in **Figure 9.15**.

2. Sites, in this context, refers to other domain controllers. Inter-Site Transports

are the mechanisms being used by your controller in the process of replicating security information to other domain controllers on your network. If you have subnetted your network, your subnets will be defined in this console.

3. There is nothing you can really do here in the context of this class, therefore close the console and move on to the next exercise.

EXERCISE 3C: ACTIVE DIRECTORY USERS AND COMPUTERS

1. Click Start>Programs>Administrative Tools>Active Directory Users and Computers. This will bring up the screen shown in **Figure 9.16**.

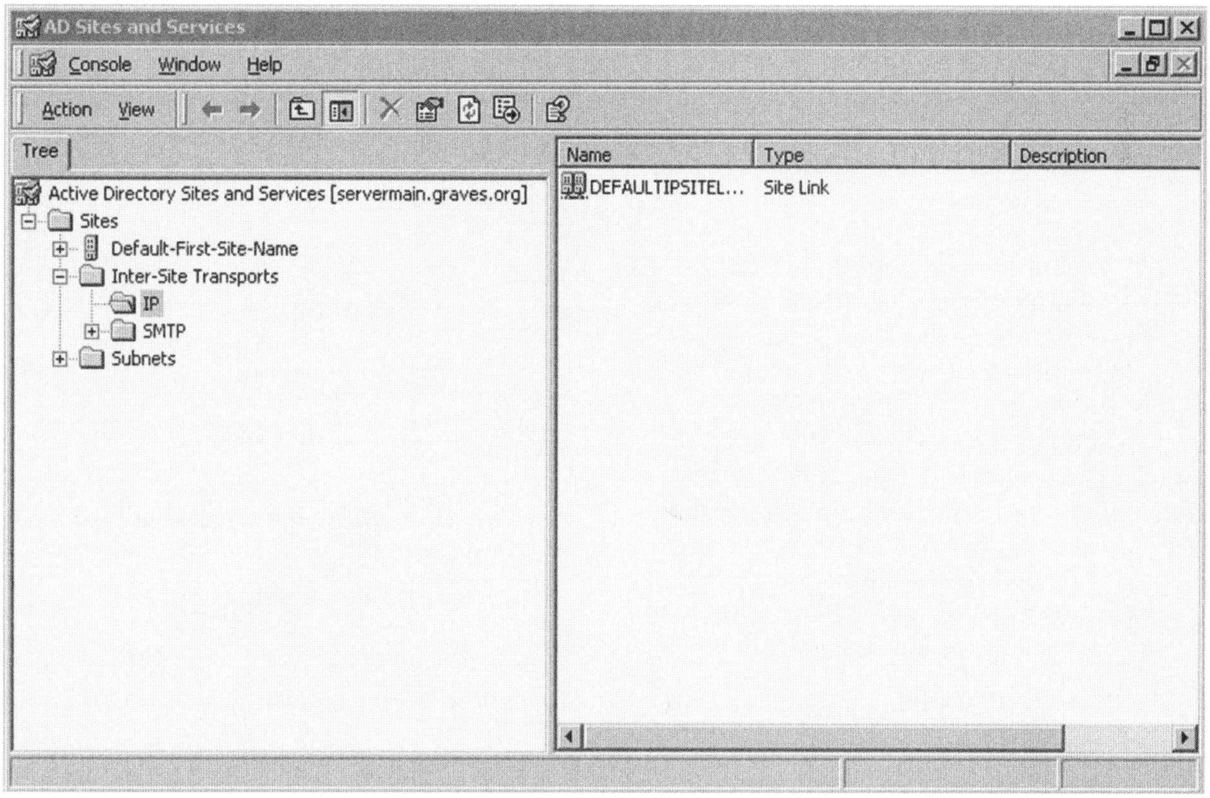

Figure 9.15 Active Directory Sites and Services

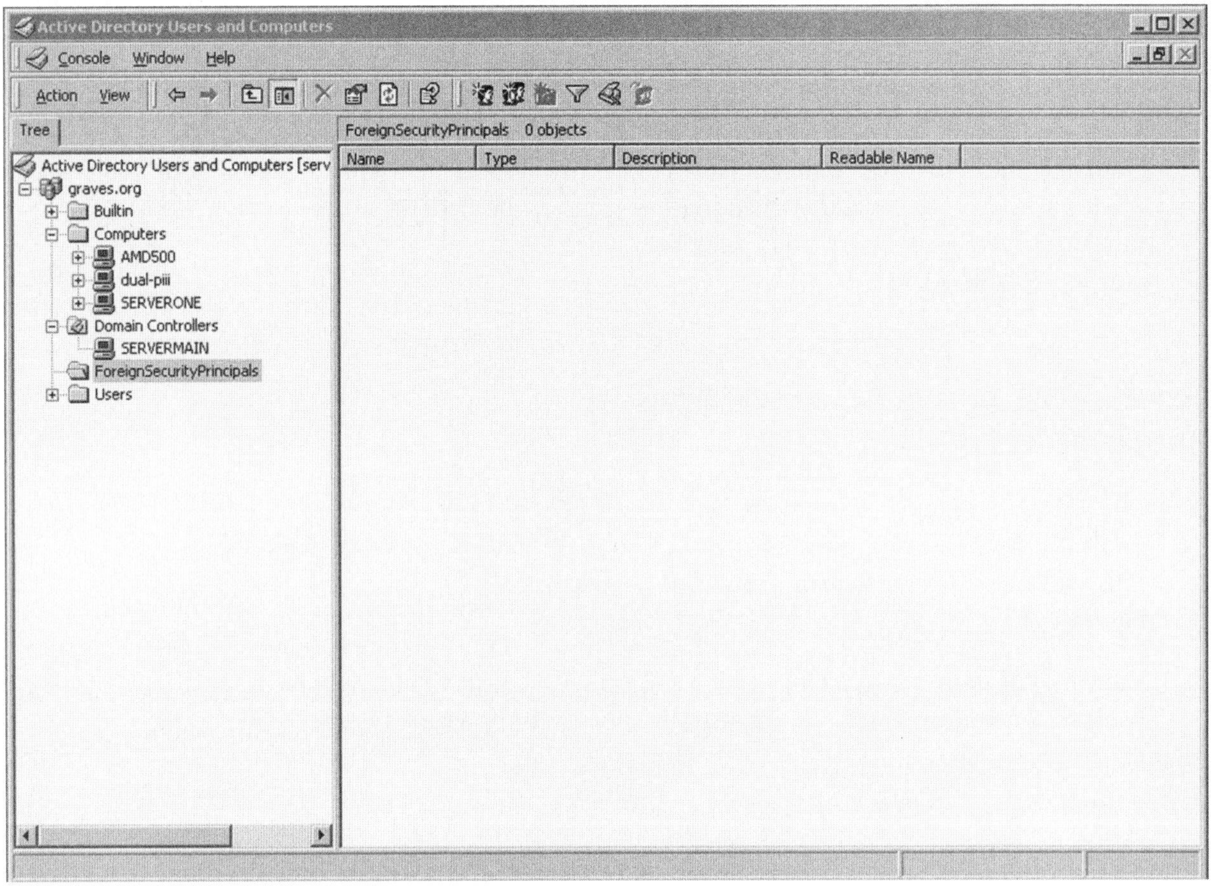

Figure 9.16 Active Directory Users and Computers

2. The five objects that can be managed in this console are:

- Builtin — These are the collective users and groups that come by default in Windows 2000 Server products.

- Computers — These are the existing computer accounts for your network. Every computer that exists on your network must have a unique account.

- Domain Controllers — This is where you add, view, and manage all domain controllers, including the local host.

- ForeignSecurityPrincipals — This is where any object from an external trusted domain is viewed or managed.

- Users — This is where you add, view, and manage users on your network.

3. Close Active Directory Users and Computers.

EXERCISE 3 DISCUSSION

1. From which Active Directory console would you manage a trust between two domains?

2. You want to change permissions assigned to the SALES group. To which Active Directory console will you go?

3. In which console are the properties of a workstation managed?

4. In which console are the properties of a server managed?

WORKING WITH NETWORK MONITOR

INTRODUCTION

Network Monitor is a tool bundled with W2KS that allows the network administrator to capture and examine individual frames as they move back and forth between the LAN and the server. The ability to do this allows the administrator to diagnose certain types of network problems.

Since a busy network will have millions of frames moving across the wire every second, there needs to be some way of picking and choosing what types of frames you want to look at. The frames intercepted and saved by Network Monitor are known as a *capture*. Network Monitor is equipped with *capture triggers* and *capture filters* that allow relatively precise selection of the types of frames that will be targeted. A capture trigger is a set of conditions that will cause some form of action to occur when those conditions are met. Capture filters are mechanisms for bringing in only the types of frames that interest you and ignoring those that don't. In this section you will get a brief overview of Network Monitor and then capture some frames for examination.

MATERIALS

- The student workstations booted to W2KS
- The W2KS CDs

NETWORK+ EXAM OBJECTIVES COVERED IN THIS LAB

3.1 Identify the basic capabilities (For example: client support, interoperability, authentication, file and print services, application support and security) of server operating systems to access network resources.

4.2 Given output from a network diagnostic utility (For example: those utilities listed in objective 4.1), identify the utility and interpret the output.

Exercise 1: Installing Network Monitor

Obviously before you can *use* Network Monitor it needs to be installed. This is not one of the services that installs by default during the original installation process, so you need to install it before you continue with the rest of the exercises in this lab.

1. Click Start>Settings>Control Panel. When Control Panel opens, double-click Add/Remove Programs. This will bring up the screen shown in **Figure 10.1**.

2. Now click Add/Remove Windows Components on the left-hand side of the window. Be patient. It can take a couple of minutes on slower machines as the Add/Remove application scans the regis-

try. When it's done, the screen you see in **Figure 10.2** will appear.

3. Scroll down until you find Management and Monitoring tools. Highlight that selection and click the Details button. The window shown in **Figure 10.3** will open.

4. Make sure the W2KS CD is in the drive and click the checkbox next to Network Monitor Tools. Click OK, which brings you back to the previous screen.

5. Now click Next. The Windows Components Wizard will begin the process of configuring Network Monitor on your server. Once again, be patient. This can take anywhere from a few minutes to the rest of your natural life. When it finishes, a screen that says Completing The

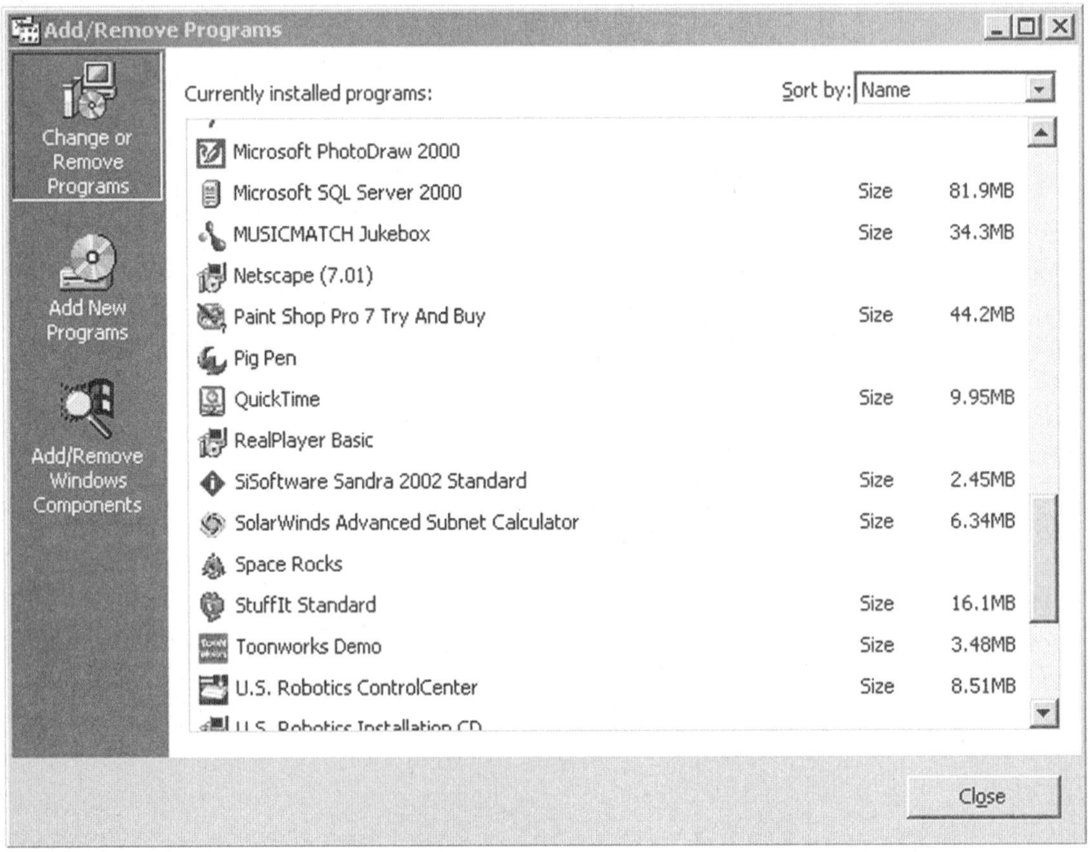

Figure 10.1 Add/Remove Programs in Windows 2000

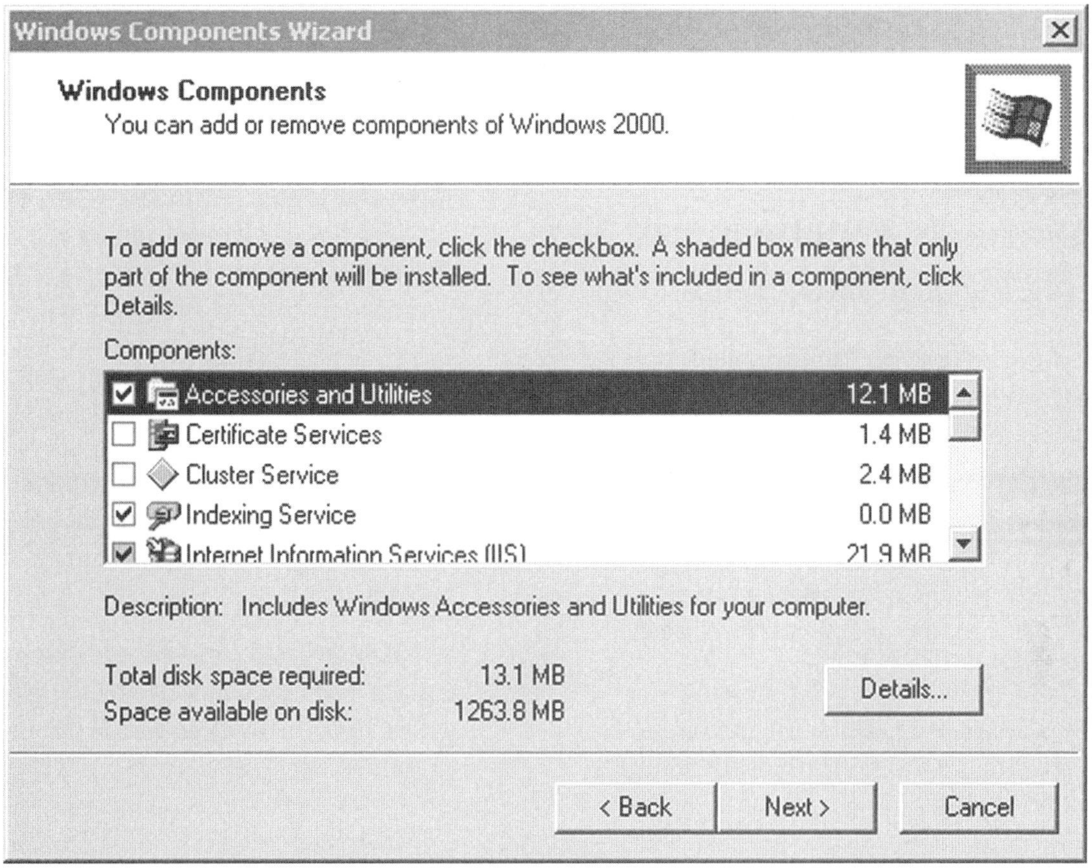

Figure 10.2 The Add/Remove Windows Components screen

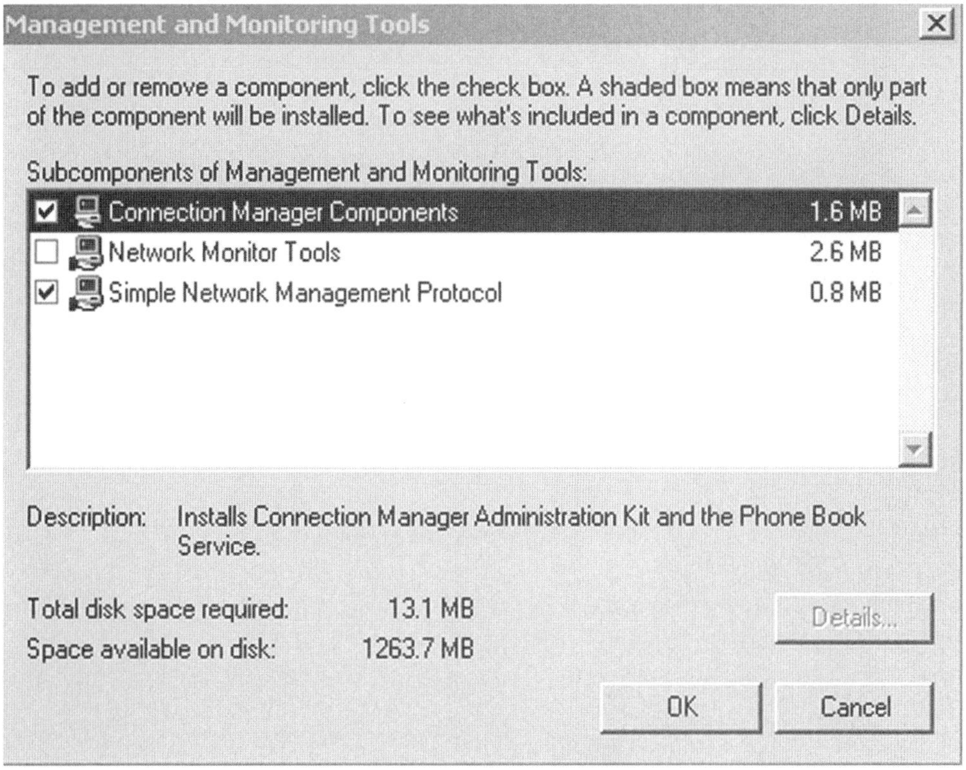

Figure 10.3 Management and Monitoring Tools Details screen

Windows Components Wizard will appear (**Figure 10.4**). Click Finish. All done.

EXERCISE 2: AN OVERVIEW OF NETWORK MONITOR

1. To open Network Monitor, click Start>Programs>Administrative Tools>Network Monitor. This will bring up the screen shown in **Figure 10.5**.

2. The menu options in this tool include:

   - File — Opens saved captures or provides the option to save a current capture.

   - Capture — Enables the capture to be configured to your needs, including triggers, filters, target addresses, and such.

   - Tools — Enables you to identify all computers running Network Monitor, locates routers on the network, provides a tool for determining the network address of a device on the network from its NetBIOS name, and provides a shortcut to Performance Monitor. (Note that not all of these tools are available without purchasing Systems Management Server).

   - Options — Enables you to configure the Network Monitor screen to your liking.

   - Window — Enables you to keep the four primary panes of Network Monitor open or to close one or more as you see fit.

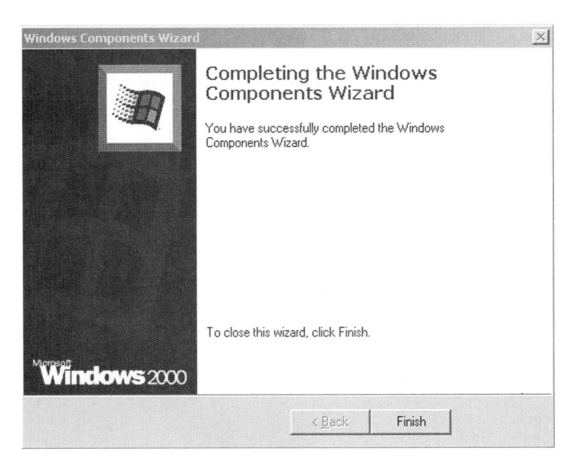

Figure 10.4   Finishing the Windows Components Wizard

- Help — Provides help on how to use specific functions within Network Monitor and provides information on the application itself.

3. You are now prompted to either select a window, or let Windows select one for you. Click Next

4. Before you begin a capture, you should set up a capture filter. Even though you have a small network set up, you don't want to have to sort through too much gobbledygook to find what you are looking for.

5. Click the Capture menu, then Filter. Note that the <F8> key is a shortcut for performing this function in the future. This will bring up a warning (**Figure 10.6**) that tells you that this version of Network Monitor only captures packets sent to or from the local computer. It also gives you some sales hype for Systems Management Server that provides

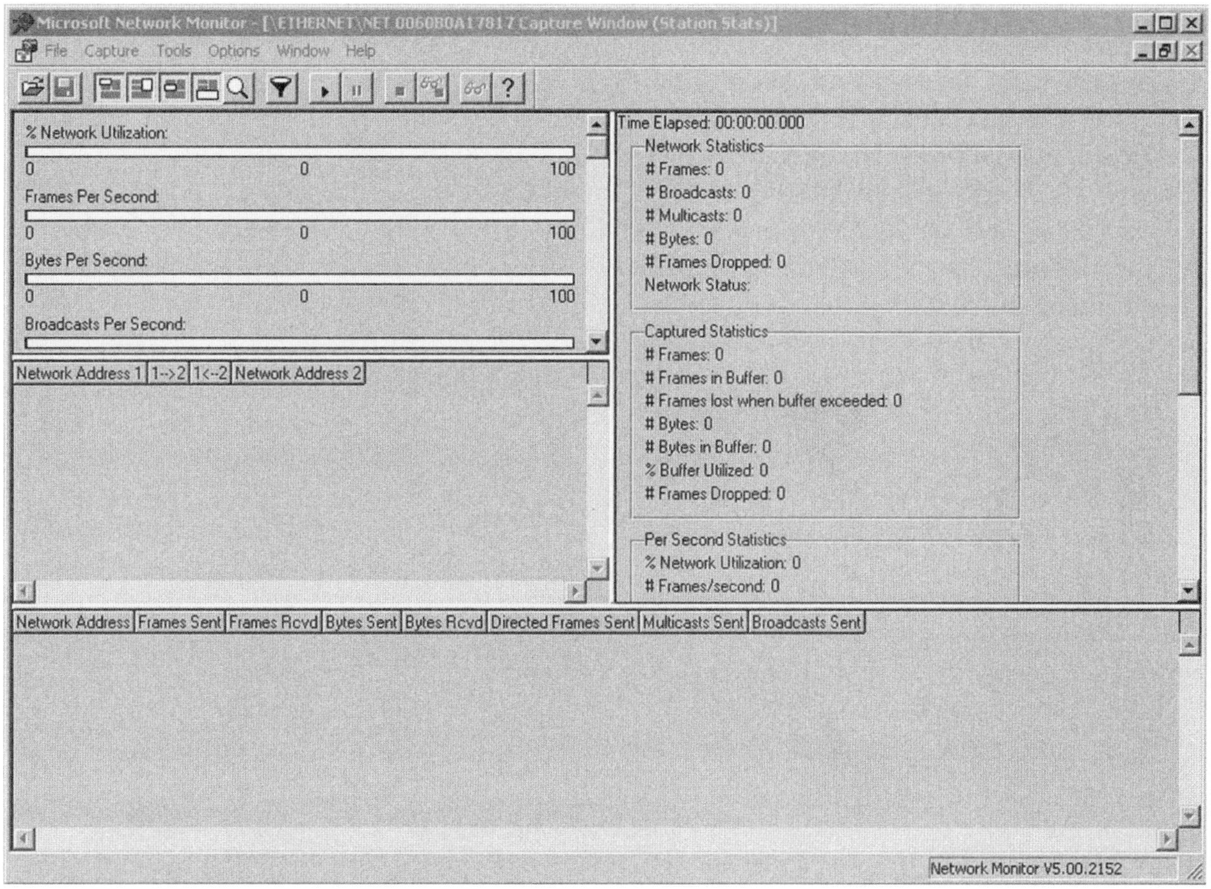

Figure 10.5 The Network Monitor Screen

Figure 10.6 Not all of the functions you see displayed in the Network Monitor menus are available unless you purchase Systems Management Server.

the ability to capture frames to or from any computer on the network.

6. Click OK and a screen like the one in **Figure 10.7** will appear. Highlight SAP/ETYPE=Any SAP or Any ETYPE and click Edit.

7. The next screen (**Figure 10.8**) allows you to select what protocols to concentrate on during your capture. Note in the Enabled Protocols window that all available protocols have been enabled. You want to pare it down a bit.

8. Click Disable All. All protocols will now appear in the Disabled Protocols window. In turn, double-click ARP, both versions of IP (but not Ipv6), NetBIOS, and TCP. Now click the Enable button. Those five protocols will now appear in the Enabled Protocols window as shown in **Figure 10.9**.

9. Click OK and then click OK on the Capture Filter screen. Now you can begin a capture.

10. Click the Capture menu, then Start. Notice that <F10> is a shortcut to this

function. After a few moments, click Capture>Stop and Display. You will get a screen similar to the one in **Figure 10.10**. Note that in this particular illustration there is a series of query requests from an address of 169.254.238.228. Running this capture helped me isolate a problem (see Sidebar on page 91).

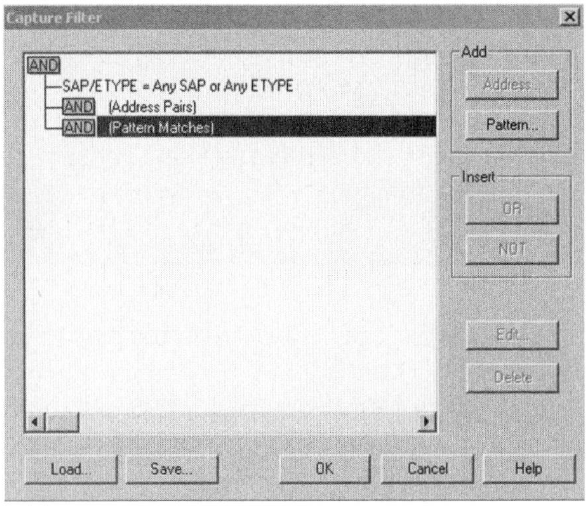

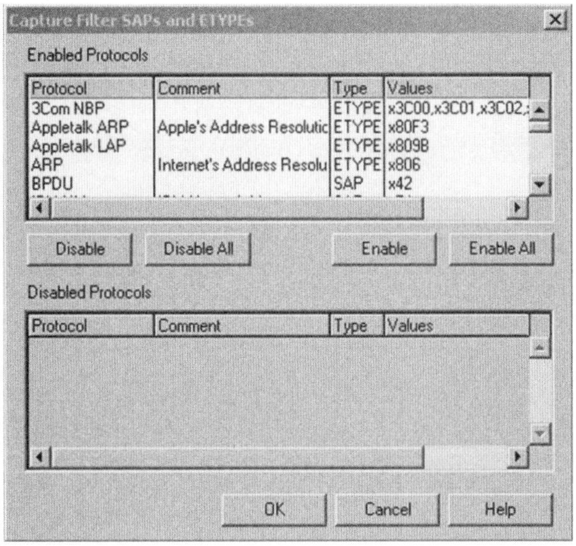

Figure 10.8 Setting up a capture filter based on protocol

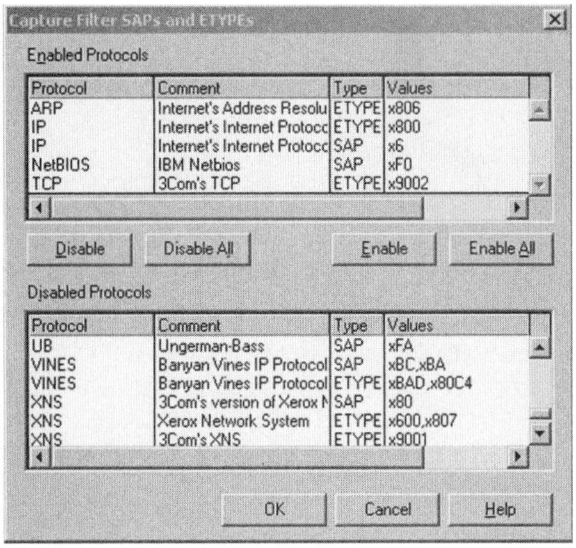

Figure 10.7 The Capture Filter screen

Figure 10.9 Selecting the protocols on which to filter

```
Microsoft Network Monitor - [Capture: 1 (Summary)]                                    _ □ ×
File  Edit  Display  Tools  Options  Window  Help                                      _ 日 ×

Frame  Time       Src MAC Addr    Dst MAC Addr   Protocol  Description                              Src Other Addr
1      3.625213   LOCAL           *BROADCAST     SMB       C transact, File = \MAILSLOT\BROWSE      SERVERMAIN
2      6.158856   00D0B70E4919    *BROADCAST     ARP_RARP  ARP: Request, Target IP: 192.168.0.110
3      6.158856   LOCAL           00D0B70E4919   ARP_RARP  ARP: Reply, Target IP: 192.168.0.2 Target H...
4      6.158856   00D0B70E4919    LOCAL          DNS       0x2BF:Std Qry for login.oscar.aol.com. of t...   192.168.0.2
5      6.158856   LOCAL           00D0B70E4919   DNS       0x2BF:Std Qry Resp. Auth. NS is . of type S...   SERVERMAIN
6      6.168871   00D0B70E4919    LOCAL          DNS       0x2C0:Std Qry for login.oscar.aol.com.grave...   192.168.0.2
7      6.168871   LOCAL           00D0B70E4919   DNS       0x2C0:Std Qry Resp. Auth. NS is graves.org....   SERVERMAIN
8      19.588167  USERCMG         *BROADCAST     SMB       C transact, File = \MAILSLOT\BROWSE      USERCMG
9      40.818695  3COM  9C2701    *BROADCAST     NBT       NS: Query req. for SERVERMAIN           169.254.238.228
10     40.888795  3COM  9C2701    *BROADCAST     NBT       NS: Query req. for GRAVES.ORG    <1C>   169.254.238.228
11     41.559760  3COM  9C2701    *BROADCAST     NBT       NS: Query req. for SERVERMAIN           169.254.238.228
12     41.629861  3COM  9C2701    *BROADCAST     NBT       NS: Query req. for GRAVES.ORG    <1C>   169.254.238.228
13     42.310840  3COM  9C2701    *BROADCAST     NBT       NS: Query req. for SERVERMAIN           169.254.238.228
14     42.380941  3COM  9C2701    *BROADCAST     NBT       NS: Query req. for GRAVES.ORG    <1C>   169.254.238.228
15     55.690079  DUAL-PIII       *BROADCAST     SMB       C transact, File = \MAILSLOT\BROWSE      DUAL-PIII
16     55.690079  DUAL-PIII       *BROADCAST     NBT       NS: Query req. for GRAVES        <1B>   DUAL-PIII
17     56.441159  DUAL-PIII       *BROADCAST     NBT       NS: Query req. for GRAVES        <1B>   DUAL-PIII
18     57.192239  DUAL-PIII       *BROADCAST     NBT       NS: Query req. for GRAVES        <1B>   DUAL-PIII
19     73.065063  DUAL-PIII       *BROADCAST     NBT       NS: Query req. for SERVERMAIN    <00>   DUAL-PIII
20     73.816143  DUAL-PIII       *BROADCAST     NBT       NS: Query req. for SERVERMAIN    <00>   DUAL-PIII
21     74.567223  DUAL-PIII       *BROADCAST     NBT       NS: Query req. for SERVERMAIN    <00>   DUAL-PIII
22     81.186741  USERCMG         *BROADCAST     DHCP      Discover          (xid=20B86707)        0.0.0.0
23     85.192501  USERCMG         *BROADCAST     DHCP      Discover          (xid=20B86707)        0.0.0.0
24     92.222610  USERCMG         *BROADCAST     DHCP      Discover          (xid=20B86707)        0.0.0.0
25     108.24...  USERCMG         *BROADCAST     DHCP      Discover          (xid=20B86707)        0.0.0.0
26     109.84...  DUAL-PIII       *BROADCAST     SMB       C transact, File = \MAILSLOT\BROWSE      DUAL-PIII
27     136.78...  LOCAL           *BROADCAST     DHCP      Inform            (xid=52D520A4)        SERVERMAIN
28     136.78...  LOCAL           *BROADCAST     DHCP      ACK               (xid=52D520A4)        SERVERMAIN
29     136.78...  3COM  032E82    *BROADCAST     DHCP      ACK               (xid=52D520A4)        192.168.0.150
30     144.79...  LOCAL           *BROADCAST     DHCP      Inform            (xid=00000000)        SERVERMAIN
31     144.79...  3COM  032E82    *BROADCAST     DHCP      ACK               (xid=00000000)        192.168.0.150

NBT Domain Name Service protocol s| F#: 14/355        Off: 42 (x2A)        L: 50 (x32)
```

Figure 10.10 A completed capture

USING NETWORK MONITOR AS A TROUBLESHOOTING TOOL

For the last few days, my wife has been after me to see why she couldn't log onto our network. Since most of the work she does really does not require that she be logged on, my priorities always managed to put this little problem on the back shelf. (You know the old saw about how the barber's kids never have a decent haircut?) While putting together this lab, I noticed that there was a machine constantly querying my server with an address of 169.254.238.228. I recognized that as an auto-configuration address a machine would assume when a DHCP server is not available to assign an address. My first thought was that there was a connectivity issue. The cable on the back of her computer was firmly in place, so I checked the patch panel. Sure enough, the cable had gotten dislodged. I had her restart her machine and sure enough, she was back on the network.

---

11. Double-clicking any given frame will allow you to view the contents. As you can see from **Figure 10.11**, the data highlighted in the bottom pane of the Network Monitor window is illegible to most people. However, in the pane above it, Network Monitor is kind enough to translate the frame for you.

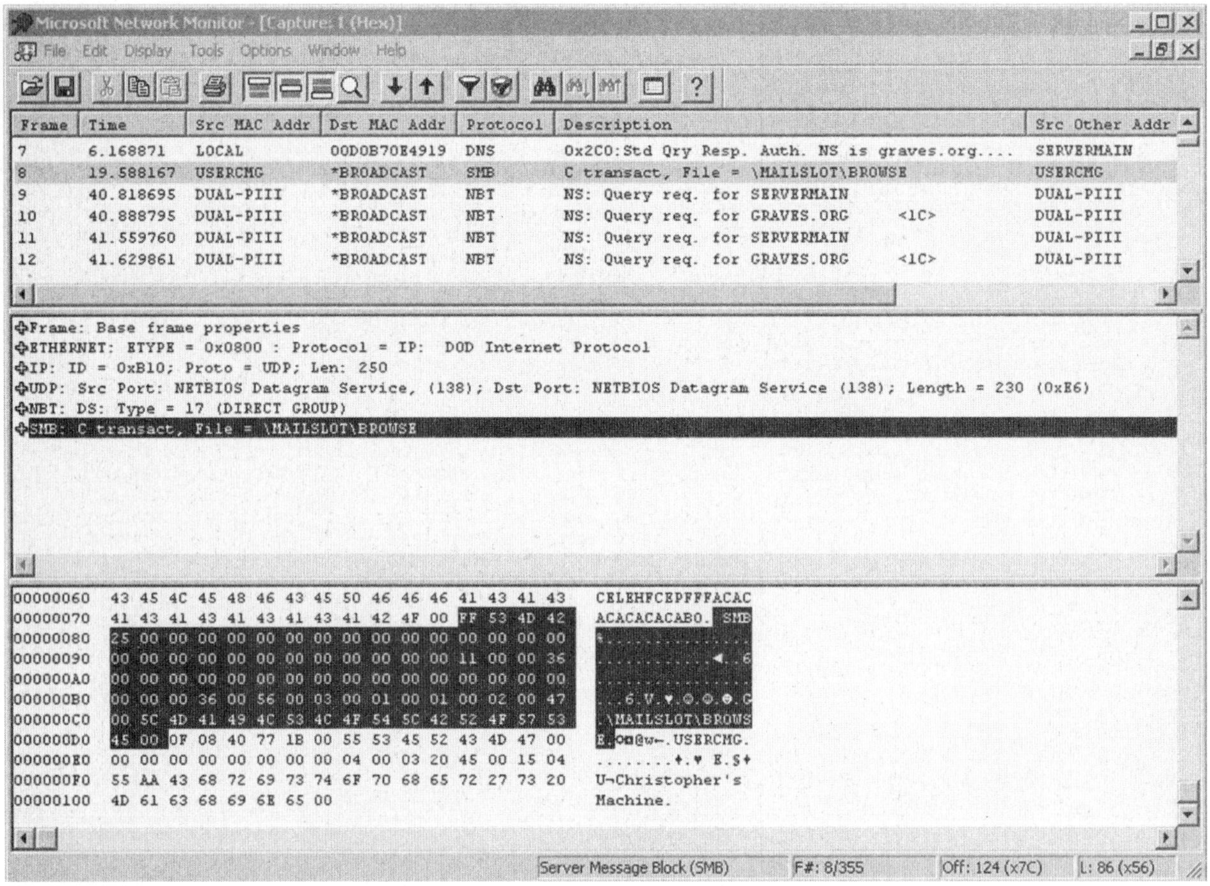

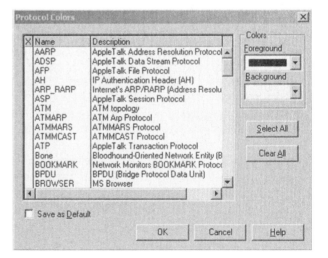

Figure 10.11   A captured frame displayed

12. Now, when you've got a lot of frames in your capture, even after setting up a decent capture filter, you want some way of quickly identifying frame types. Network Monitor provides a way.

13. Click the Display menu, and select Colors. You'll now have the screen shown in **Figure 10.12**. Place an X in the checkbox next to ARP/RARP, and in the Colors section, select green as the foreground color. Click OK.

14. Now all ARP frames in your capture stand out against the others, because they show up in bright green text (see **Figure 10.13**).

Figure 10.12   Each protocol can be set to display in a different color.

Frame	Time	Src MAC Addr	Dst MAC Addr	Protocol	Description	Src Other Addr
47	304.32...	CAROL-2XT...	*BROADCAST	NBT	NS: Registration req. for GRAVES <00>	CAROL-2XTZYW7S7
48	305.07...	CAROL-2XT...	*BROADCAST	NBT	NS: Registration req. for GRAVES <00>	CAROL-2XTZYW7S7
49	305.73...	DUAL-PIII	*BROADCAST	DHCP	Discover (xid=32210B00)	0.0.0.0
50	305.82...	CAROL-2XT...	*BROADCAST	NBT	NS: Registration req. for GRAVES <00>	CAROL-2XTZYW7S7
51	306.58...	CAROL-2XT...	*BROADCAST	NBT	NS: Registration req. for GRAVES <00>	CAROL-2XTZYW7S7
52	309.79...	CAROL-2XT...	*BROADCAST	NBT	NS: Registration req. for CAROL-2XTZYW7S7<03>	CAROL-2XTZYW7S7
53	310.19...	CAROL-2XT...	*BROADCAST	NBT	NS: Query req. for GRAVES <1C>	CAROL-2XTZYW7S7
54	310.19...	LOCAL	*BROADCAST	ARP_RARP	ARP: Request, Target IP: 192.168.0.8	
55	310.19...	CAROL-2XT...	LOCAL	ARP_RARP	ARP: Reply, Target IP: 192.168.0.110 Target...	
56	310.19...	LOCAL	CAROL-2XT...	NBT	NS: Query (Node Status) resp. for GRAVES ...	SERVERMAIN
57	310.19...	CAROL-2XT...	*BROADCAST	Netlogon	SAM LOGON request from client	CAROL-2XTZYW7S7
58	310.19...	CAROL-2XT...	LOCAL	Netlogon	SAM LOGON request from client	CAROL-2XTZYW7S7
59	310.19...	CAROL-2XT...	*BROADCAST	Netlogon	SAM LOGON request from client	CAROL-2XTZYW7S7
60	310.19...	CAROL-2XT...	LOCAL	Netlogon	SAM LOGON request from client	CAROL-2XTZYW7S7
61	310.24...	LOCAL	CAROL-2XT...	Netlogon	Unknown Type	SERVERMAIN
62	310.29...	CAROL-2XT...	*BROADCAST	NBT	NS: Query req. for SERVERMAIN	CAROL-2XTZYW7S7
63	310.29...	LOCAL	CAROL-2XT...	NBT	NS: Query (Node Status) resp. for SERVERMAI...	SERVERMAIN
64	310.29...	CAROL-2XT...	LOCAL	TCP	....S., len: 0, seq:3499450142-349945014...	CAROL-2XTZYW7S7
65	310.29...	LOCAL	CAROL-2XT...	TCP	.A..S., len: 0, seq:2643218274-264321827...	SERVERMAIN
66	310.29...	CAROL-2XT...	LOCAL	TCP	.A...., len: 0, seq:3499450143-349945014...	CAROL-2XTZYW7S7
67	310.29...	CAROL-2XT...	LOCAL	NBT	SS: Session Request, Dest: SERVERMAIN ...	CAROL-2XTZYW7S7
68	310.29...	LOCAL	CAROL-2XT...	NBT	SS: Positive Session Response, Len: 0	SERVERMAIN
69	310.30...	CAROL-2XT...	LOCAL	SMB	C negotiate, Dialect = NT LM 0.12	CAROL-2XTZYW7S7
70	310.30...	LOCAL	CAROL-2XT...	SMB	R negotiate, Dialect # = 5	SERVERMAIN
71	310.33...	CAROL-2XT...	*BROADCAST	NBT	NS: Query req. for GRAVES.ORG <1C>	CAROL-2XTZYW7S7
72	310.43...	CAROL-2XT...	*BROADCAST	NBT	NS: Registration req. for CAROL-2XTZYW7S7	CAROL-2XTZYW7S7
73	310.47...	CAROL-2XT...	LOCAL	TCP	.A...., len: 0, seq:3499450352-349945035...	CAROL-2XTZYW7S7
74	310.54...	CAROL-2XT...	*BROADCAST	NBT	NS: Registration req. for CAROL-2XTZYW7S7<03>	CAROL-2XTZYW7S7
75	310.73...	DUAL-PIII	*BROADCAST	DHCP	Discover (xid=32210B00)	0.0.0.0
76	311.08...	CAROL-2XT...	*BROADCAST	NBT	NS: Query req. for GRAVES.ORG <1C>	CAROL-2XTZYW7S7
77	311.18...	CAROL-2XT...	*BROADCAST	NBT	NS: Registration req. for CAROL-2XTZYW7S7	CAROL-2XTZYW7S7

Figure 10.13 Selecting a different color for a specific protocol allows it to stand out from the rest.

EXERCISE 2 DISCUSSION

1. What do you call the data that is collected after running Network Monitor for a while?

2. How can you limit the types of packets you view to those of a single workstation?

3. What kinds of properties can you use to filter the packets you snag off the wire?

Working with the Performance Applet

Introduction

Another valuable tool that is part of the W2KS package is Performance. An evolutionary offset of an earlier tool Microsoft called Performance Monitor, Performance is broken down into two separate tools. The System Monitor allows the administrator to collect and view data on a number of hardware-related issues, such as CPU, memory, and disk performance. Performance Logs and Alerts collects data about these performance issues and can be configured to notify the administrator if a particular value exceeds the threshold defined. I think you're going to like this lab.

Materials

For this lab, you need the student machines booted to W2KS.

Network+ Exam Objectives Covered in this Lab

3.1 Identify the basic capabilities (For example: client support, interoperability, authentication, file and print services, application support and security) of server operating systems to access network resources.

4.2 Given output from a network diagnostic utility (For example: those utilities listed in objective 4.1), identify the utility and interpret the output.

Exercise 1: Running System Monitor

System Monitor is able to track your server's performance in some very specific areas. All together, the number of different statistics, or *counters,* as Microsoft calls them, measures in the hundreds. It is far beyond the scope of this book to explore every one of those, so I will concentrate on a select few that provide the administrator with valuable information about server hardware performance. Properly used, this information can tell you when your server needs more memory, an additional processor, or even if your network needs to be subnetted. In the following exercise, you will be looking at some CPU and memory issues and play a quick game of Pinball.

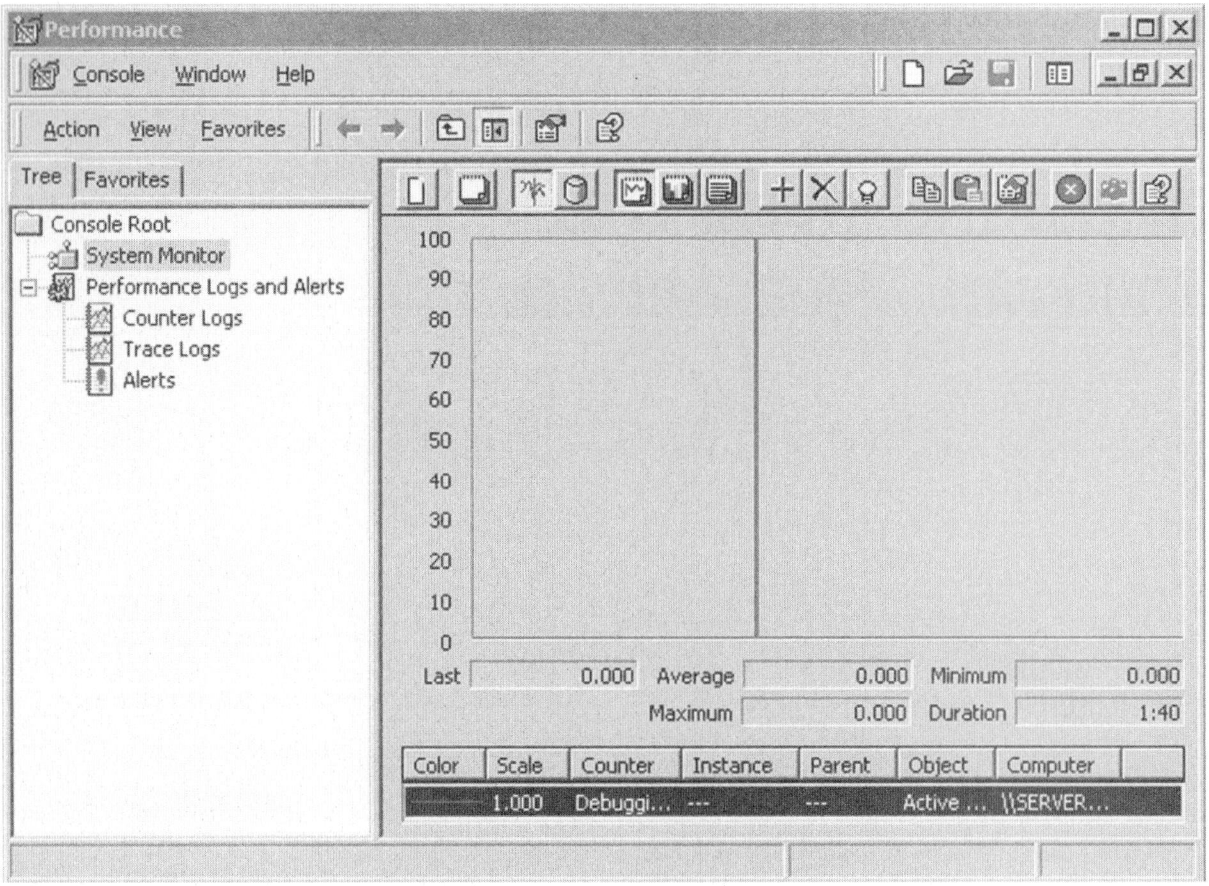

Figure 11.1 The Performance Console Window

1. To begin with, click Start> Programs>Administrative Tools>Performance. This will bring up the Performance Console shown in **Figure 11.1**.

2. Note that the left-hand pane of the window has two subfolders. One is System Monitor (and should be highlighted by default) and the other is Performance Logs and Alerts. Leave System Monitor highlighted.

3. Right-click anywhere in the right-hand pane and from the pop-up menu that appears, select Add Counters. A screen like the one in **Figure 11.2**

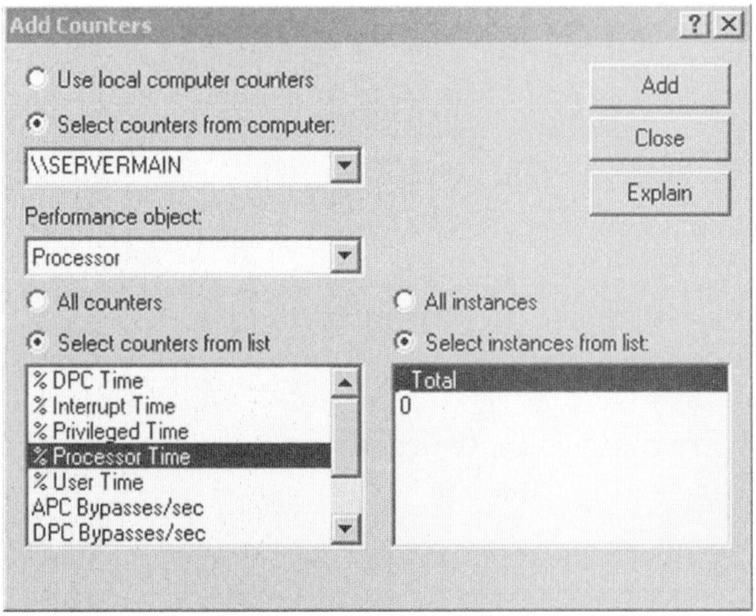

Figure 11.2 Adding counters to System Monitor

will appear. Note that there are *performance objects* and there are *performance counters*. By default, Performance always opens with the Processor object selected.

4. With the counter % Processor Time highlighted, click the Explain button. Microsoft provides a detailed explanation for each of its counters (**Figure 11.3**). Use the scroll bar to read the entire explanation of what this counter means. Now spend a few moments looking at some of the various performance objects and the different counters each one provides. Don't try to explore all of them. You would still be doing this lab sometime next week!

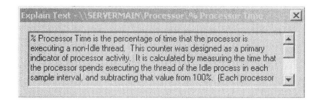

Figure 11.3 Microsoft provides detailed explanations for each of its counters.

5. Now you will add some counters to a log that you are going to collect. Be sure to view the explanation of each counter as you add it.

- From the Processor object, add % Processor Time, % User Time, and % Interrupt Time.

- Now, in the Performance Object field, scroll up until you find Memory. From here, select Pages/Sec (the default highlighted counter), Page Reads/Sec, Page Writes/Sec, and Page Faults/Sec.

- In the Performance Object field, scroll down until you find the Process object. Select % Processor Time and % User Time.

NOTE: There is a big difference between the Processor object and the Process object. The Processor object collects data on what is going on inside of the processor itself, regardless of who or what is using the processor. The Process object collects information of specific threads of code that are running in the processor.

While both of these objects have counters named % Processor Time and % User Time, these counters are collecting different types of information. In the Processor object, % Processor Time tells you how much CPU performance is being used at any instant. That same counter in the Process object tells you what percentage of processor utilization is being caused by a specific process. Note in the Process object, on the lower right-hand pane, you can select specific processes to monitor.

6. Click Close and let Performance begin to collect data. Now you'll give the system a real workout. Click Start>Programs> Accessories>Games>Pinball. Play about two minutes worth of Pinball. You can start a new game by pressing <F2>. Use <Z> for your left-hand paddle and <?/> for the right-hand paddle. (Note to instructor: If you don't keep a tight lid on this particular exercise, this lab can easily take several hours. And you can send your thanks that I did not specify for the computers to have speakers to me through Delmar.)

7. Close Pinball and compare scores. The winner explains what all these counters mean to rest of the class.

8. Examine your different counters and take a look at the resources this inane little game ties up (see **Figure 11.4**). Now, for the rest of your career, you'll understand why we don't let people play Pinball on the server. (Hopefully, you'll also wonder, as I so often have, why they include a game like that on a serious server product to begin with!)

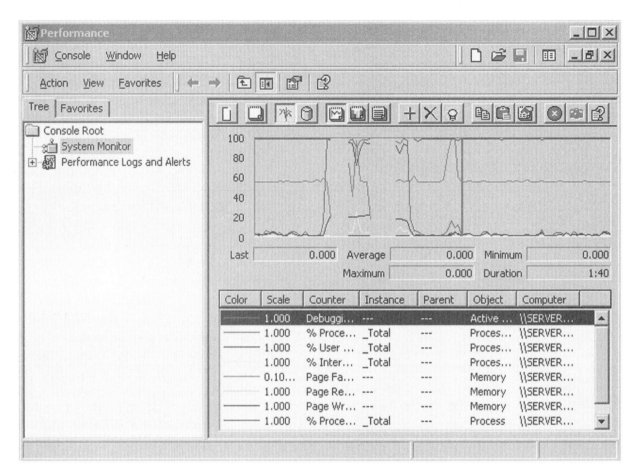

Figure 11.4   An example of data collected by System Monitor

EXERCISE 1 DISCUSSION

1. What are the two functions of the Performance applet?

2. What types of data can System Monitor collect?

3. How do you think System Monitor might help diagnose a hardware problem?

EXERCISE 2: WORKING WITH PERFORMANCE LOGS AND ALERTS

In the next exercise, you are going to see how you can program your server to monitor itself over time. You will create a performance log,

collect data for a few minutes, and then open the log file to seen what you have collected.

1. Open the performance console (if it's not already open).

2. Double-click Performance Logs and Alerts.

3. Highlight Counter Logs and then, somewhere in the right-hand pane of the Performance console, right-click and select New Log Settings. You will be prompted to fill in a name for your new log. Use CLASS1. Click OK

4. Now, as you did when you explored System Monitor, you need to add some counters to your new log. Select from the Processor object % Processor Time and % User Time, and from the Memory

Object select Pages/sec, Page Faults/sec, and Page Reads/sec. Click Apply and then OK.

5. Your new log should now appear in the right-hand pane. Double-click it to bring up its properties.

6. Click General and set the Sample Data field to five seconds. Click Log Files and make a note of the path to your newly created log file. You're going to want it later. Click OK.

7. Now play Pinball for a couple more minutes. (See? I told you that you were going to like this lab!)

8. Now, to see the results of your log, in the Performance console highlight System Monitor. Over in the right-hand pane, right-click in an empty area and select Properties.

9. Click the Source tab and browse to the log file you created. Click Time Range. Select the entire range and click Apply.

10. Then, as you see on the next screen, there's nothing there. To view the data, you need to do one more thing. Go back to the Properties screen of System Monitor. Click the Data tab. Click Add.

11. Select all the counters from the Memory object, then use the pull-down menu to select the Processor object. Add those counters and click Close. Click Apply and then OK. You now have the chart for the log you generated.

EXERCISE 2 DISCUSSION

1. What is the purpose of creating a Performance Log?

2. If you suspect your server is in need of a memory upgrade, what different processes might you want to log?

3. If you suspect your server is in need of a CPU upgrade, what different processes might you want to log?

EXERCISE 3: SETTING AN ALERT

Performance logging by itself is a valuable tool. However, it can be made even more powerful by having Performance notify you when a certain counter exceeds a certain point. Here's how to do that.

1. In the Performance console, double-click Performance Logs and Alerts. Highlight Alerts and in the right-hand pane, right-click in an empty spot. Select New Alert Settings.

2. In the box that pops up (**Figure 11.5**), name your new settings ALERT1.

Figure 11.5 Each new alert you add needs a unique name in the system.

3. This will bring up the screen shown in **Figure 11.6**. Add all of the same counters you did in the previous exercise. From the Processor object, select % Processor Time and % User Time. From the Memory Object, you want Pages/sec, Page Faults/sec, Page Reads/sec, and Page Writes/sec.

4. Where it says Alert when the value is, in turn, highlight each counter, and where it says "under," change the value to "over." Fill in the value of 80 for each of the two

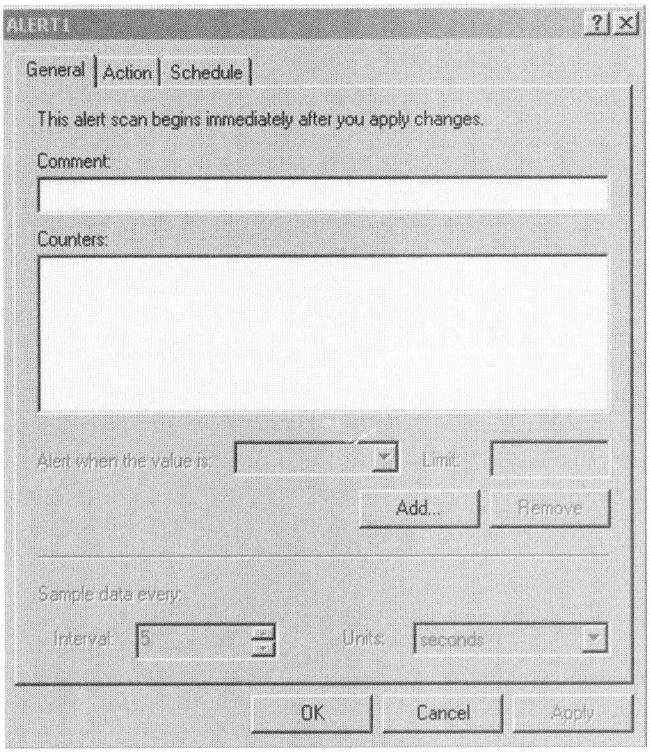

Figure 11.6 You add counters to your alerts in a manner similar to that of performance logging.

processor values and 5 for each of the memory items.

5. Click the Action tab (**Figure 11.7**) and click the checkbox next to Send a network message to, and in the field type in `administrator`. Leave Log an entry in the application event log checked as well. You'll look at that log in the next lab.

6. Click Apply and OK. Within a few seconds you should be barraged with messages like the one in **Figure 11.8**. If not, play a few more minutes of Pinball. (Heh, heh. You won't even get the game *started* before System Monitor starts hammering you!)

7. To stop the alerts from coming in, right-click ALERT1 and select Stop. You'll probably have quite a few alert screens to close.

EXERCISE 3 DISCUSSION

1. How does a Performance Alert differ from a Performance Log?

2. What is an unwanted effect of setting the Alert threshold too high or too low?

3. Where are two different places to which you can direct Performance Alerts?

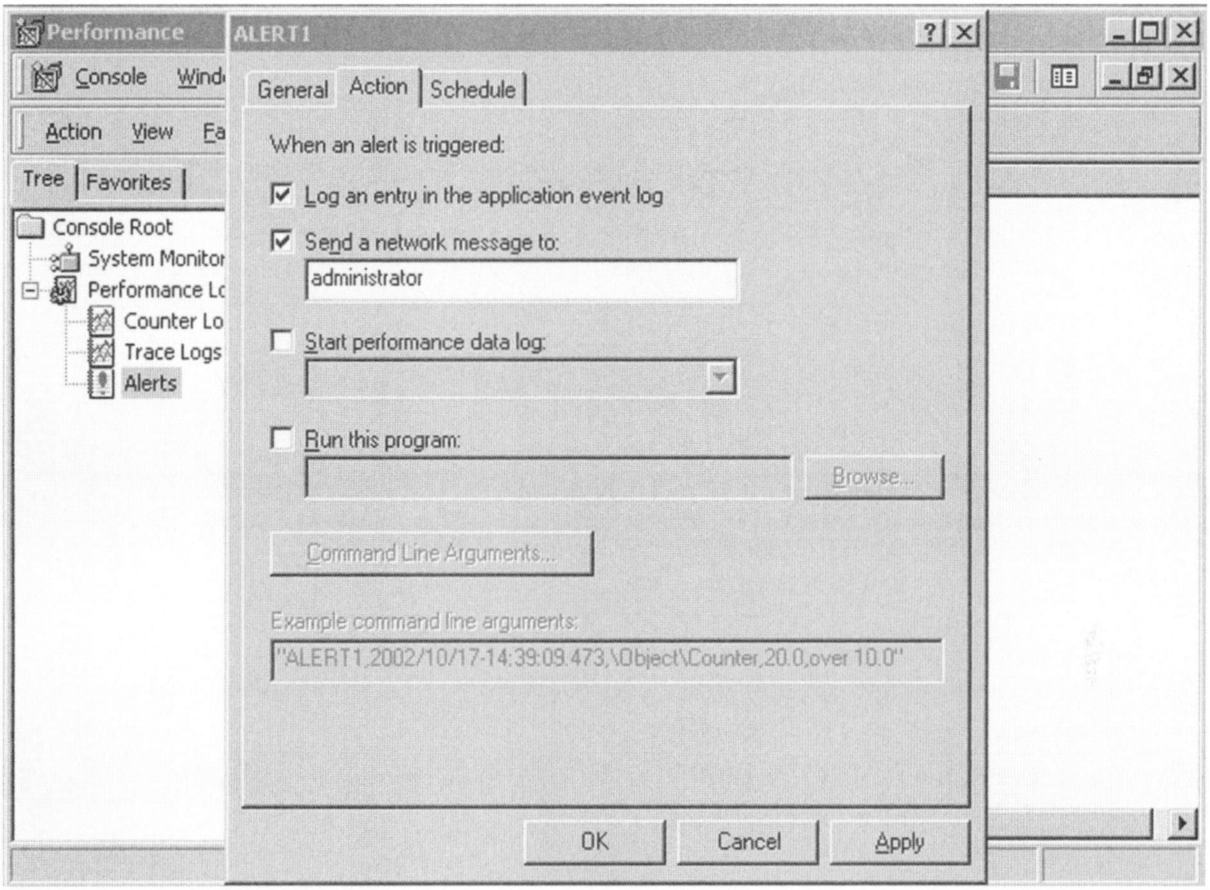

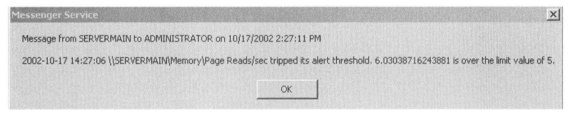

Figure 11.7 Alerts can be logged in the application log or sent directly to a user on the network.

Figure 11.8 An example of an alert sent directly to a user

THE EVENT VIEWER

INTRODUCTION

One of the better troubleshooting tools provided by W2KS is called *Event Viewer*. Event Viewer collects information on different activities that are generated by either hardware or software action. These events range from benign to critical, and Event Viewer frequently can provide information that helps the administrator diagnose what led up to the event.

Event Viewer reports three degrees of severity in its logs. See **Table 12.1** for a description.

With this information in mind, it's time to take a look at Event Viewer and see what there is to find.

Table 12.1   Event Viewer Severity Classifications

Symbol	Severity	Description
	Information	Describes the successful operation of an application, driver, or service
	Error	A significant problem, such as loss of data or loss of functionality
	Warning	An event that is not necessarily significant, but may indicate a possible future problem

MATERIALS

For this lab, all you need are the Student Machines booted to W2KS.

NETWORK+ EXAM OBJECTIVES COVERED IN THIS LAB

3.1 Identify the basic capabilities (For example: client support, interoperability, authentication, file and print services, application support and security) of server operating systems to access network resources.

4.2 Given output from a network diagnostic utility (For example: those utilities listed in objective 4.1), identify the utility and interpret the output.

EXERCISE 1: AN OVERVIEW OF EVENT VIEWER

1. Click on Start>Programs>Administrative Tools>Event Viewer. The Screen in **Figure 12.1** will appear. Here, I added a computer that had not been on my network since rebuilding the domain. That gave us some very interesting errors to examine.

2. Notice in the left-hand pane, there are six different aspects of system performance that are logged. These are as follows:

   - Application Log — Here is where events logged by applications or programs are recorded.

   - Security Log — Events such as invalid logon attempts are recorded here. If

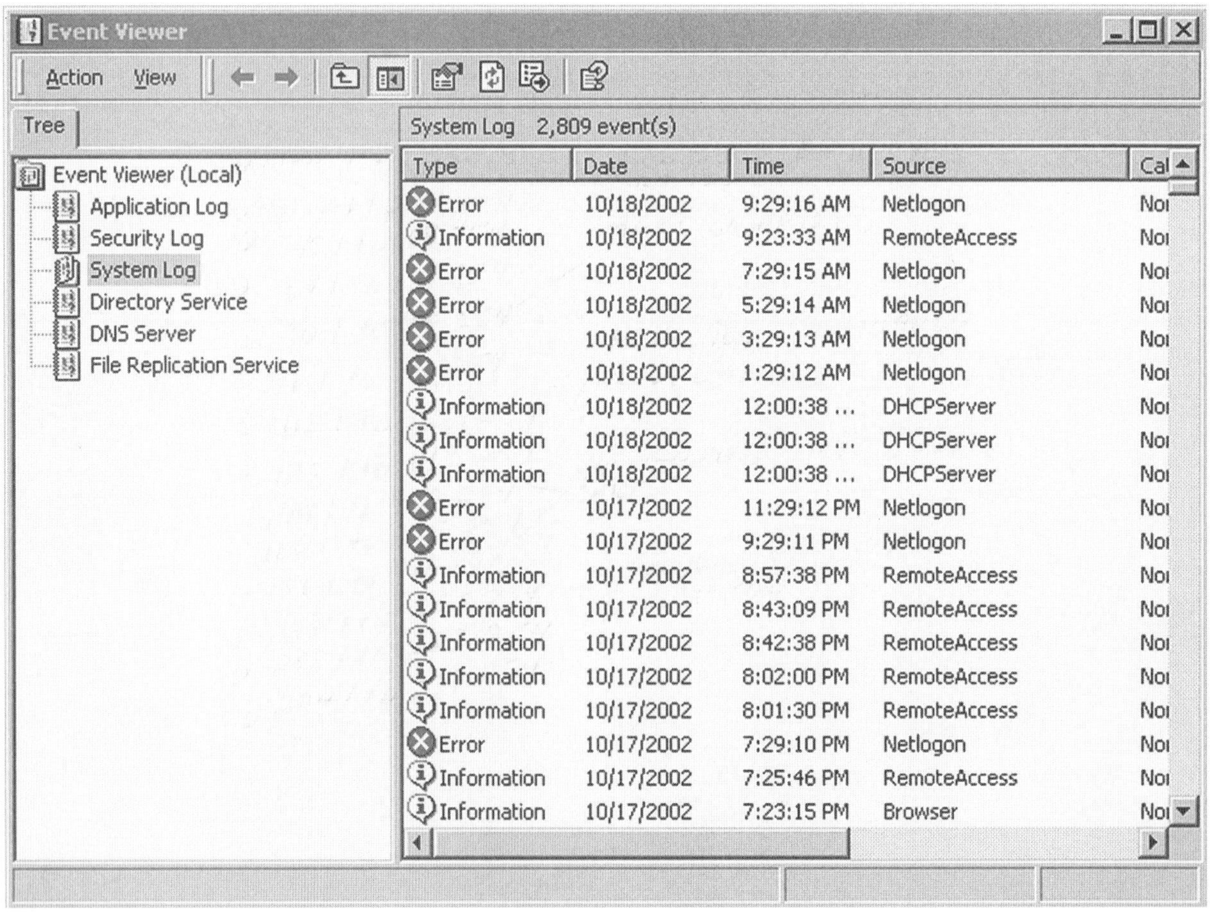

Figure 12.1   The Event Viewer screen

you have auditing enabled, this is where auditing events will be stored.

- System Log — Any event generated by a system component, whether it be hardware (such as a memory error) or OS related, will be stored here.

- Directory Service Log — Events directly related to Active Directory are recorded here.

- DNS Server — Events generated by DNS services are stored here.

- File Replication Service — As its name implies, events generated by the File Replication Service are stored here. An example of this event would be the failure of two domain control-lers to successfully replicate the SID or SYSVOL.

3. Highlight the Application Log in the left-hand pane. Click Action. Click Properties. This will bring up the screen in **Figure 12.2**. The two tabs in this screen are General and Filter. Under General, you can configure several different things.

4. Under Display Name, change Application Log to Server Applications. Click Apply. Notice the change on your Event Viewer Screen.

5. Now change the Application Log back to its original name. Notice that the default Maximum log size is 512KB. Also, by default, when the log size exceeds 512KB, it is set to Overwrite events older than seven days. If hard drive space is not an issue, I suggest that your log should be increased to 2048KB (2MB) and that you

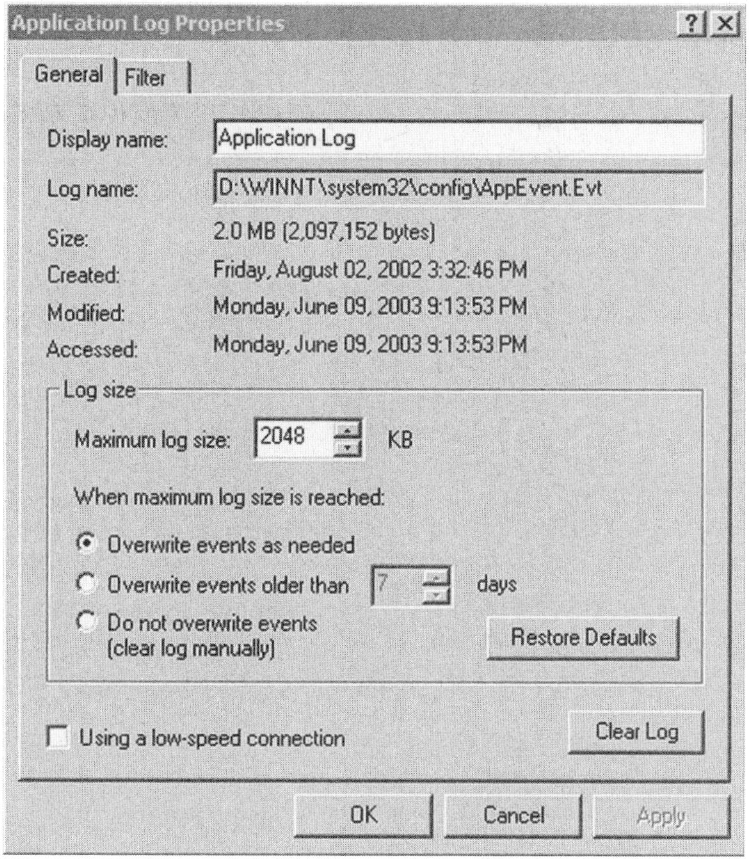

Figure 12.2 Application Log Properties

select the option Overwrite events as needed. Go ahead and make these changes.

6. Another option on this screen is Clear log. Clicking this button will completely delete all events recorded in this log. You will be asked if you want to save the log files before you continue (**Figure 12.3**). You don't really want to clear your log, so click Cancel and move on.

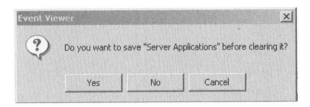

Figure 12.3 Unless you know for certain there is critical data in your old logs, there isn't much point in saving them when you clear the log.

EXERCISE 1 DISCUSSION

1. Where would you find the Event Viewer in Windows 2000?

2. If a service fails to start, what kind of icon will Event Viewer display?

3. You have configured your server to audit failed logon attempts. Where would reports of these events be logged?

TROUBLESHOOTING THE NOS THROUGH EVENT VIEWER

When you are first getting starting with this network administration thing, it can appear to be overwhelming. You'll soon get over that. You'll find that all providers of network operating systems provide a substantial amount of support for their product. In Windows 2000 and XP, the Event Viewer provides information on what caused a failure. If this information isn't helpful by itself, you can take it a step further and make use of the TechNet services on Microsoft's Web page (currently at http://www.microsoft.com/technet/). A search of key words from the message is very likely to bring up several articles related to your problem. Novell offers very similar services and Linux help can be obtained from Red Hat, Mandrake, and numerous other Linux vendors.

Another good resource for Microsoft users is the Windows 2000 or Windows XP Resource Guide. Again, Novell provides similar references for its NOS. In the Resource Guide you will find reams of information. Nearly every error message generated by the NOS is explained, and most causes of service or driver failure can be found in this guide. These are not inexpensive books, but compared to the cost of your NOS and/or the cost of the administrator's time, the resource guide is an essential tool for any administrator.

EXERCISE 2: ANALYZING AN EVENT

1. For this exercise, go to the System Log. This is where you will find the most events. Since it is impossible for me to predict what all of your systems are going to look like, follow closely with the illustration in addition to performing these steps on your own computer. My descriptions of events and other information will be based entirely on the illustration.

2. Double-click any error your System Log may be reporting. If there are no errors, find an Information event. Lacking that, double-click any event but follow the text carefully. Double-clicking any event will bring up the Event Properties screen (**Figure 12.4**).

3. If you are looking at an error message, such as the one in the illustration, the description screen will tell you precisely what failed. In the case of the error in the

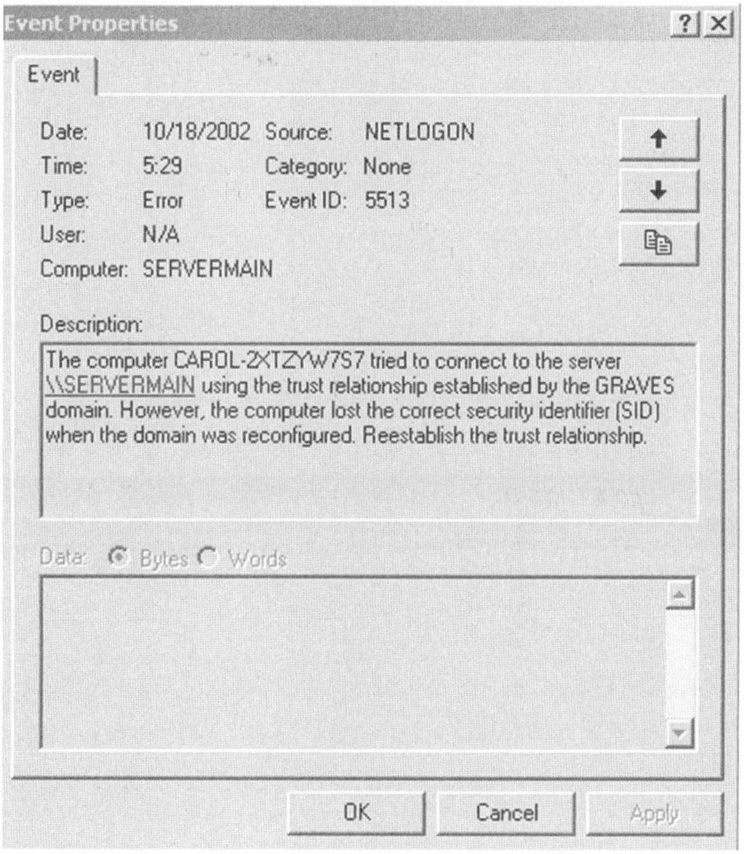

Figure 12.4 The Event Properties Screen

illustration, I am even told how to fix the problem. All I need to do is rejoin this computer to the domain. (See Lab Seven for details on adding a computer account to the domain.)

4. Close Event Viewer.

EXERCISE 2 DISCUSSION

1. What kinds of information can you learn from an event if you double-click it?

2. If a service fails to start, what can you learn by examining the event?

AN OVERVIEW OF SUBNETTING

INTRODUCTION

Subnetting is one of those subjects that, for some reason, has a tendency to drive beginning students more than a little mad. Once you get the hang of it, it isn't that difficult. The thing to remember is that it's all mathematics. Now for some, that's going to make this a little more intimidating than it ever would have been. But relax. It's simple math.

MATERIALS

The only materials you'll need for this lab are a pencil, lots of erasers, and some paper.

> *NOTE:* For the following exercises, follow along in Chapter Twelve, Using TCP/IP on the Network.

NETWORK+ EXAM OBJECTIVES COVERED IN THIS LAB

2.5 Identify the components and structure of IP (Internet Protocol) addresses (IPv4, IPv6) and the required setting for connections across the Internet.

2.6 Identify classful IP (Internet Protocol) ranges and their subnet masks (For example: Class A, B and C).

2.7 Identify the purpose of subnetting.

2.8 Identify the differences between private and public network addressing schemes.

4.5 Given a troubleshooting scenario between a client and the following server environments, identify the cause of a stated problem.

EXERCISE 1: HOW MANY SUBNETS DO YOU NEED?

In **Figure 13.1**, count the number of total networks you will need to successfully subnet this organization.

EXERCISE 2: SUBNETTING A NETWORK

1. Using the network address of 148.120.0.0 as your starting point, calculate the correct subnet mask that will give the minimum number of acceptable subnets for the above network.

   How many networks are you going to need? _____

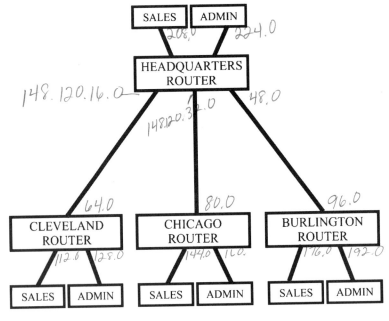

Figure 13.1

2. Next, figure out the following parameters for each of your subnets:

- Network address of subnet

- Address range of subnet

- The number of possible hosts on each subnet *12 bits*

- The broadcast address of each subnet

Write your results in the space below.

255.255.240.0

```
148.120.16.0 -16.1 to 31.254
148.120.32.0 - 32.1 to 47.254
148.120.48.0 - 48.1 to 63.254      HEADQUARTERS
148.120.64.0 - 64.1 to 79.254
148.120.80.0 - 80.1 to 95.254
148.120.96.0 - 96.1 to 111.254    } CLEVELAND
148.120.112.0 - 112.1 to 127.254
148.120.128.0 - 128.1 to 143.254
148.120.144.0 - 144.1 to 159.254  } CHICAGO
148.120.160.0 - 160.1 to 175.254
148.120.176.0 - 176.1 to 191.254
148.120.192.0 - 192.1 to 207.254  } BURLINGTON
148.120.208.0 - 208.1 to 223.254
148.120.224.0 - 224.1 to 239.254
```

THE TCP/IP UTILITIES

INTRODUCTION

Any computer that has TCP/IP installed as a networking protocol can benefit from several different utilities that are part of the package. It doesn't matter what NOS you use. These utilities are part of the TCP/IP suite, whether you use Linux, Microsoft, or Novell. There are quite a number of utilities bundled with the suite. I'll be looking at the top five in this lab. The ones I examine are:

- Ping
- ARP
- Tracert
- Ipconfig
- Route

Some of these utilities are provided as troubleshooting tools. Some are communications, reporting, and file transfer mechanisms. They all have two things in common; they are all part of TCP/IP, and a good network administrator needs to be comfortable with all of them.

MATERIALS

For this lab, you need to start all the student workstations as W2K Pro machines. Internet access is useful, but not necessary.

NETWORK+ EXAM OBJECTIVES COVERED IN THIS LAB

4.1 Given a troubleshooting scenario, select the appropriate network utility.

EXERCISE 1: WORKING WITH PING

Ping is a utility that calls on the services of the *Internet Control Messaging Protocol* (ICMP) to function. The primary function of ICMP is to return error messages to a transmitting device whenever the data that is being sent runs into problems. Network administrators have come to rely on Ping so heavily that they sometimes take it for granted. Here, you will look at some of the uses of Ping.

Figure 14.1 The Windows 2000 command line utility

1. Ping is best run from a command prompt. Click Start>Run and in the command line, type cmd. This will bring up what is euphemistically referred to as a DOS window (**Figure 14.1**).

2. If the instructor's machine was configured according to the instructions outlined in the introduction to this manual, the address of that machine should be 192.168.0.110. Have each student type ping 192.168.0.110. This will result in one of two screens.

3. The screen shown in **Figure 14.2** is the result of a successful ping. From this you can pull out three useful pieces of information.

   • bytes — the number of bytes of data that were in the packet sent from the transmitting device to the sending device and that were in the reply

   • time — the amount of time that passed between the transmission request and receipt of the reply

   • TTL — the *time to live* specified in the IP header of the echo-reply packet

4. **Figure 14.3** is one example of an unsuccessful ping. You can replicate this screen by attempting to ping a nonexistent address on your own network. The application tells us the packet timed out. This is an unfortunate reply in that it actually tells us nothing, other than that you weren't able to ping the target device. This could be because the TTL specified in the header was too short, because the target address wasn't found on the network, or even that the transmitting device is not properly configured on the network. You can rule out the TTL issue in the next step.

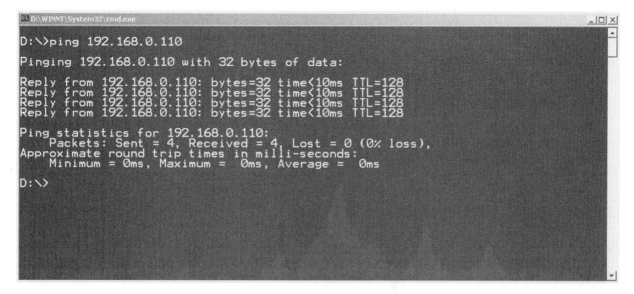

Figure 14.2   The results of a successful ping

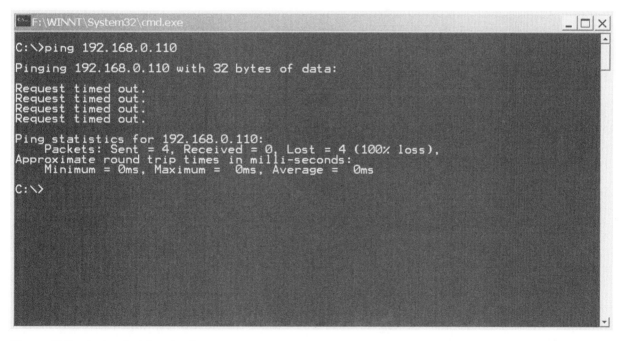

Figure 14.3   A ping that timed out

5. At the command prompt, type
   `ping 192.168.0.110 -w 10000`
   (**Figure 14.4**). This trigger specifies a
   TTL of 10,000ms. This is a much
   higher value that any network device
   would ever be configured for. If you still
   get the timed out error message, you
   know the TTL is not too short. This
   most likely points at a configuration or
   hardware error.

113

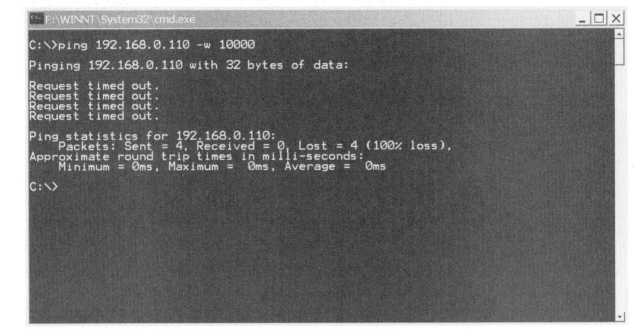

Figure 14.4 The TTL of the ICMP packets can be configured to be as long as you need.

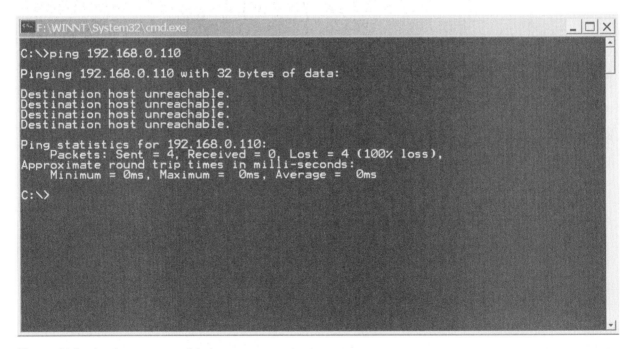

Figure 14.5 Another unsuccessful ping message

6. Another unsuccessful ping is illustrated in **Figure 14.5**. This message is a bit more useful. You can replicate this screen by attempting to ping an address outside your network. It suggests that the system was unable to properly route the packets. This can be the result of a failed connection between the transmitting or the receiving host and your switch, router, or hub. It can also indicate that no available routing tables were able to resolve the target address.

```
D:\WINNT\System32\cmd.exe                                                  _ | □ | x |
Reply from 192.168.0.110: bytes=32 time<10ms TTL=128
Reply from 192.168.0.110: bytes=32 time<10ms TTL=128
Reply from 192.168.0.110: bytes=32 time<10ms TTL=128
Reply from 192.168.0.110: bytes=32 time<10ms TTL=128
Reply from 192.168.0.110: bytes=32 time<10ms TTL=128
Reply from 192.168.0.110: bytes=32 time<10ms TTL=128
Reply from 192.168.0.110: bytes=32 time<10ms TTL=128
Reply from 192.168.0.110: bytes=32 time<10ms TTL=128
Reply from 192.168.0.110: bytes=32 time<10ms TTL=128
Reply from 192.168.0.110: bytes=32 time<10ms TTL=128
Reply from 192.168.0.110: bytes=32 time<10ms TTL=128
Reply from 192.168.0.110: bytes=32 time<10ms TTL=128
Reply from 192.168.0.110: bytes=32 time<10ms TTL=128
Reply from 192.168.0.110: bytes=32 time<10ms TTL=128
Reply from 192.168.0.110: bytes=32 time<10ms TTL=128
Reply from 192.168.0.110: bytes=32 time<10ms TTL=128

Ping statistics for 192.168.0.110:
    Packets: Sent = 31, Received = 31, Lost = 0 (0% loss),
Approximate round trip times in milli-seconds:
    Minimum = 0ms, Maximum =  0ms, Average =  0ms
Control-C
^C
D:\>
```

Figure 14.6   The results of a continuous ping

7. By default, Ping only sends out four echo requests and waits for four replies. Sometimes, in order to test the integrity of your circuit (for example, if you suspect a bad hub or a noisy signal), you would like to see the results of a lot more packets going back and forth.

8. At the command prompt, type `ping 192.168.0.110 –t` and watch what happens. As you see, Ping sends a continuous stream of echo requests to the target address.

9. Press <Ctrl-C>. This will break the continuous ping and report on the screen how many packets were sent, what percentage were successful, and the minimum, maximum, and average durations of the round trip (see **Figure 14.6**).

10. For a complete listing of the triggers available to the Ping command, type `ping /?` at the command prompt.

EXERCISE 1 DISCUSSION

1. What TCP/IP protocol does Ping rely on for its services?

2. By default, how many packets does Ping send out? How can you make it send an unlimited number?

3. If your Ping attempts are timing out, how can you increase the time to live for your packets?

EXERCISE 2: USING ARP

The *Address Resolution Protocol* provides another useful utility called ARP (conveniently enough). The ARP utility makes use of the ARP protocol to identify the MAC address of a device as long as you know either the NetBIOS name or the IP address of the device in question.

1. Open a command prompt once again (if it's not already open). Type `cls` in order to clear the screen. You don't want any clutter confusing the issue.

2. Now ping as many other computers on your network as you can in about a minute. I'll explain the reason for the hurry in a moment.

3. Now, type `arp –a` at the command prompt. You should get a screen like the

```
F:\WINNT\System32\CMD.exe                                                    _ |□| x|

F:\>arp -a

Interface: 192.168.0.26 on Interface 0x1000003
  Internet Address       Physical Address      Type
  192.168.0.8            00-50-da-0b-64-38      dynamic
  192.168.0.16           00-10-5a-03-2e-82      dynamic
  192.168.0.110          00-60-b0-a1-78-17      dynamic

F:\>
```

Figure 14.7   The ARP utility allows you to resolve a computer's MAC address from its IP address.

```
F:\WINNT\System32\CMD.exe                                                    _ |□| x|

F:\>arp -a

Interface: 192.168.0.26 on Interface 0x1000003
  Internet Address       Physical Address      Type
  192.168.0.8            00-50-da-0b-64-38      dynamic
  192.168.0.16           00-10-5a-03-2e-82      dynamic
  192.168.0.110          00-60-b0-a1-78-17      dynamic

F:\>arp -a
No ARP Entries Found

F:\>
```

Figure 14.8   The ARP cache is only good for two minutes.

one in **Figure 14.7**. Regardless of whether you pinged by NetBIOS name or IP address, ARP will return the IP address and the physical (or MAC) address, and tell you whether that address is statically or dynamically configured. In other words, is that host a DHCP client or not?

4. Wait about three minutes and press <F3> to reenter the previous command.

If you waited long enough, you should be informed that no ARP entries were found (**Figure 14.8**). This is because these entries are kept in the *ARP cache*. All entries are flushed after two minutes.

5. For a complete listing of the triggers available to the ARP command, type arp /? at the command prompt.

```
D:\WINNT\System32\cmd.exe
D:\>tracert www.delmar.com

Tracing route to www.delmar.com [198.80.136.29]
over a maximum of 30 hops:

  1   110 ms    91 ms   100 ms  arc0.wnskvtao.sover.net [216.114.155.2]
  2   100 ms   100 ms    91 ms  216.114.154.60
  3   100 ms    90 ms    90 ms  207.136.212.234
  4   110 ms   100 ms   110 ms  c0p1-0.nycmny83.sover.net [207.136.206.202]
  5   120 ms   110 ms   100 ms  paix-ny-1.inpr.core.algx.net [198.32.118.9]
  6   110 ms   100 ms   111 ms  FAST7-0.NYCMNY8347W.core.algx.net [216.99.231.34
]
  7   130 ms   131 ms   130 ms  cvg3-core1-s3-1.atlas.algx.net [165.117.65.141]

  8   131 ms   130 ms   661 ms  206.181.193.14
  9   130 ms   130 ms   141 ms  bgp1-g1-0-0.core.fuse.net [216.68.6.12]
 10   130 ms   140 ms   140 ms  Thomson-Learning-DS3-gw-S6-1-0.bgp1.core.fuse.ne
t [216.68.230.146]
 11   130 ms   141 ms   130 ms  198.80.143.10
 12   140 ms     *      140 ms  198.80.143.52
 13   140 ms   140 ms   141 ms  198.80.136.29

Trace complete.

D:\>
```

Figure 14.9 Tracert finds each hop between the transmitting machine and the intended recipient.

EXERCISE 2 DISCUSSION

1. What is the primary purpose of ARP?
2. How can you view the ARP cache?
3. How long does the ARP cache stay alive?

EXERCISE 3: WORKING WITH TRACERT

This exercise is best done if you have Internet access. However, you can make it work on a local network as well. My illustrations will be based on an Internet connection.

1. Open a command prompt.
2. Tracert works with IP addresses, NetBIOS names, or domain names. If you have Internet access, type `tracert www.delmar.com`. If not, replace the Delmar domain with one of the NetBIOS names for a computer on your network. You will get a screen similar to the one in **Figure 14.9** either way. Tracing a route over the Internet, however, will return considerably more entries than the single entry you would get on a LAN.
3. Examine the results carefully. Notice that for each entry there are three different round-trip times listed. Tracert works by sending three separate ICMP echo-request packets, each with an increasingly longer TTL. You're seeing the results of each of those requests. In the last column you will see the name of each domain through which your packets traveled and the IP address of each interface they encountered.
4. For a complete listing of the triggers available to the Tracert command, type `tracert /?` at the command prompt.

EXERCISE 3 DISCUSSION

1. What can Tracert tell you about the status of your network?
2. How does Tracert do what it does, and how many packets does it send out?

```
D:\WINNT\System32\cmd.exe                                          _|□|×|

D:\>ipconfig

Windows 2000 IP Configuration

Ethernet adapter Local Area Connection:

        Connection-specific DNS Suffix  . :
        IP Address. . . . . . . . . . . : 192.168.0.110
        Subnet Mask . . . . . . . . . . : 255.255.255.0
        Default Gateway . . . . . . . . :

PPP adapter Sovernet:

        Connection-specific DNS Suffix  . :
        IP Address. . . . . . . . . . . : 216.114.181.165
        Subnet Mask . . . . . . . . . . : 255.255.255.255
        Default Gateway . . . . . . . . : 216.114.181.165

D:\>
```

Figure 14.10 A simple Ipconfig report

EXERCISE 4: USING IPCONFIG

Another tool heavily used by administrators is Ipconfig. This utility can return a substantial amount of information regarding each interface on a machine. In addition, if DHCP is used on your network, Ipconfig can be used to release and renew IP addresses assigned by DHCP. Here's a look at how it works.

1. Open a command prompt.

2. Type `ipconfig` at the command prompt. This will return a screen like the one in **Figure 14.10**. In this illustration both my NIC and my modem were active. As a result, Ipconfig returned information on both. Your screen will most likely return information only about the NIC.

3. As you can see, Ipconfig returns only a limited amount of information when used with no triggers. You learn the IP address, subnet mask, and any installed default gateways, and that's about it. For a more detailed report, type `ipconfig –all` at the command prompt. This will return the results in **Figure 14.11**.

4. Examine Figure 14.11 carefully. As you see, there is a substantial amount of additional information supplied. You learn the NetBIOS name of the computer, the domain of which it is a member, and whether routing and proxy are enabled. For each interface, in addition to IP address, subnet mask, and gateway, you also learn the MAC address and the DNS servers bound to TCP/IP.

5. Now clear your screens. Look at how Ipconfig assists the DHCP process. If the student machines are all booted to W2K Pro, they should be configured as DHCP clients. Any machines (except the instructor machine) running W2KS should be rebooted to Pro.

6. At the command prompt, type `ipconfig –release` (**Figure 14.12**). This will flush any IP information from your NIC. Now type `ipconfig –all` again. The IP address and the subnet mask are now both listed as 0.0.0.0, and you can no longer browse the network.

7. Type `ipconfig –renew` (**Figure 14.13**). You are now assigned an IP address and

```
D:\WINNT\System32\cmd.exe                                              _ | □ | x |
D:\>ipconfig -all

Windows 2000 IP Configuration

        Host Name . . . . . . . . . . . . : servermain
        Primary DNS Suffix  . . . . . . . : graves.org
        Node Type . . . . . . . . . . . . : Hybrid
        IP Routing Enabled. . . . . . . . : No
        WINS Proxy Enabled. . . . . . . . : No
        DNS Suffix Search List. . . . . . : graves.org

Ethernet adapter Local Area Connection:

        Connection-specific DNS Suffix  . :
        Description . . . . . . . . . . . : HP Ethernet with LAN remote power ad
apter
        Physical Address. . . . . . . . . : 00-60-B0-A1-78-17
        DHCP Enabled. . . . . . . . . . . : No
        IP Address. . . . . . . . . . . . : 192.168.0.110
        Subnet Mask . . . . . . . . . . . : 255.255.255.0
        Default Gateway . . . . . . . . . :
        DNS Servers . . . . . . . . . . . : 127.0.0.1

PPP adapter Sovernet:

        Connection-specific DNS Suffix  . :
        Description . . . . . . . . . . . : WAN (PPP/SLIP) Interface
        Physical Address. . . . . . . . . : 00-53-45-00-00-00
        DHCP Enabled. . . . . . . . . . . : No
        IP Address. . . . . . . . . . . . : 216.114.181.165
        Subnet Mask . . . . . . . . . . . : 255.255.255.255
        Default Gateway . . . . . . . . . : 216.114.181.165
        DNS Servers . . . . . . . . . . . : 209.198.87.24
                                            209.198.87.40
```

Figure 14.11   A detailed Ipconfig report

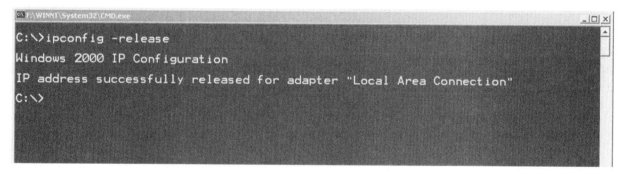

```
F:\WINNT\System32\CMD.exe                                              _ | □ | x |
C:\>ipconfig -release

Windows 2000 IP Configuration

IP address successfully released for adapter "Local Area Connection"

C:\>
```

Figure 14.12   Using Ipconfig to dump the TCP/IP bindings from a NIC

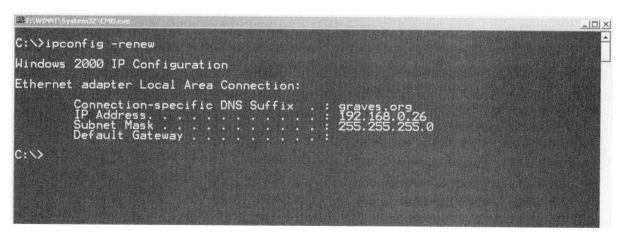

```
F:\WINNT\System32\CMD.exe                                              _ | □ | x |
C:\>ipconfig -renew

Windows 2000 IP Configuration

Ethernet adapter Local Area Connection:

        Connection-specific DNS Suffix  . : graves.org
        IP Address. . . . . . . . . . . . : 192.168.0.26
        Subnet Mask . . . . . . . . . . . : 255.255.255.0
        Default Gateway . . . . . . . . . :

C:\>
```

Figure 14.13   Refreshing the TCP/IP configuration of a NIC using Ipconfig

```
D:\WINNT\System32\cmd.exe                                                    _|□|X|

D:\>route print
==============================================================================
Interface List
0x1 ...........................  MS TCP Loopback interface
0x1000003 ...00 60 b0 a1 78 17 .......  AMD PCNET Family Ethernet Adapter
0xa000004 ...00 53 45 00 00 00 .......  WAN (PPP/SLIP) Interface
==============================================================================
==============================================================================
Active Routes:
Network Destination        Netmask          Gateway       Interface  Metric
        0.0.0.0          0.0.0.0    216.114.180.124  216.114.180.124     1
      127.0.0.0        255.0.0.0        127.0.0.1        127.0.0.1        1
    192.168.0.0    255.255.255.0    192.168.0.110    192.168.0.110        1
  192.168.0.110  255.255.255.255      127.0.0.1        127.0.0.1          1
  192.168.0.255  255.255.255.255    192.168.0.110    192.168.0.110        1
  216.114.155.1  255.255.255.255  216.114.180.124  216.114.180.124        1
216.114.180.124  255.255.255.255      127.0.0.1        127.0.0.1          1
216.114.180.255  255.255.255.255  216.114.180.124  216.114.180.124        1
      224.0.0.0        224.0.0.0    192.168.0.110    192.168.0.110        1
      224.0.0.0        224.0.0.0  216.114.180.124  216.114.180.124        1
255.255.255.255  255.255.255.255    192.168.0.110    192.168.0.110        1
Default Gateway:     216.114.180.124
==============================================================================
Persistent Routes:
  None

D:\>
```

Figure 14.14   Results of the route print command

subnet mask (and any other configuration data DHCP has been programmed to assign). Don't be surprised if you wind up with the same address you had before. Whenever possible, DHCP will keep the same address for any given machine even when addresses are renewed.

8. For a complete listing of the triggers available to the ipconfig command, type `ipconfig /?` at the command prompt.

EXERCISE 4 DISCUSSION

1. What kind of information do you get from simply typing `ipconfig` at the command prompt?

2. How do you get a more detailed report?

3. Your administrator has just changed the IP address of your default gateway and configured DHCP to assign it to DHCP clients. What is the fastest way for your users to immediately start using the new gateway?

EXERCISE 5: USING THE ROUTE COMMAND

Any W2KS machine can be configured to be a router as well as a server. Even those that aren't maintained as routers keep both static and dynamic entries in the local routing table. The route command can be a useful tool for administrators because it allows users to either view or edit the routing tables on a local server.

1. To view the current routing tables for a local machine, type `route print` at the command prompt. This will bring up a screen similar to the one in **Figure 14.14**. This is a listing of all the entries to the current routing table.

2. For a complete listing of all the different triggers available to the Route command, type `route /?` at the command prompt.

BACKUP AND RECOVERY

INTRODUCTION

In the following exercises, you are going to get a brief overview of the Windows 2000 Backup utility. Then you'll go through the process of performing a backup and subsequently deleting and restoring the data you backed up.

MATERIALS

Optimally, in order to do this lab, each computer should be equipped with a tape backup unit. However, I have to assume that is not the case in the majority of classrooms and that the backup will be done to file in these exercises.

> *NOTE:* This lab maps to Chapter Sixteen, Data Recovery and Fault Tolerance, in the book.

NETWORK+ EXAM OBJECTIVES COVERED IN THIS LAB

3.1 Identify the basic capabilities (For example: client support, interoperability, authentication, file and print services, application support and security) of the following server operating systems to access network resources.

3.11 Identify the purpose and characteristics of fault tolerance.

3.12 Identify the purpose and characteristics of disaster recovery.

EXERCISE 1: AN OVERVIEW OF THE BACKUP UTILITY

1. To start W2K Backup, click Start>Programs>Accessories>System Tools>Backup. This will bring up the screen shown in **Figure 15.1**.

2. The three options shown in this window are Backup Wizard, Restore Wizard, and Emergency Repair Disk. You won't be working with any of the Wizards in this lab. You'll be learning to do manual backup and recovery.

3. Click the Backup tab. You should now have a window like that in **Figure 15.2**. Note that you can back up any or all of your local drives, from your CD-ROM drive, from the System State, and from Network Places. If you click your C (or any other) drive, Backup will show the various folders on that drive. You can

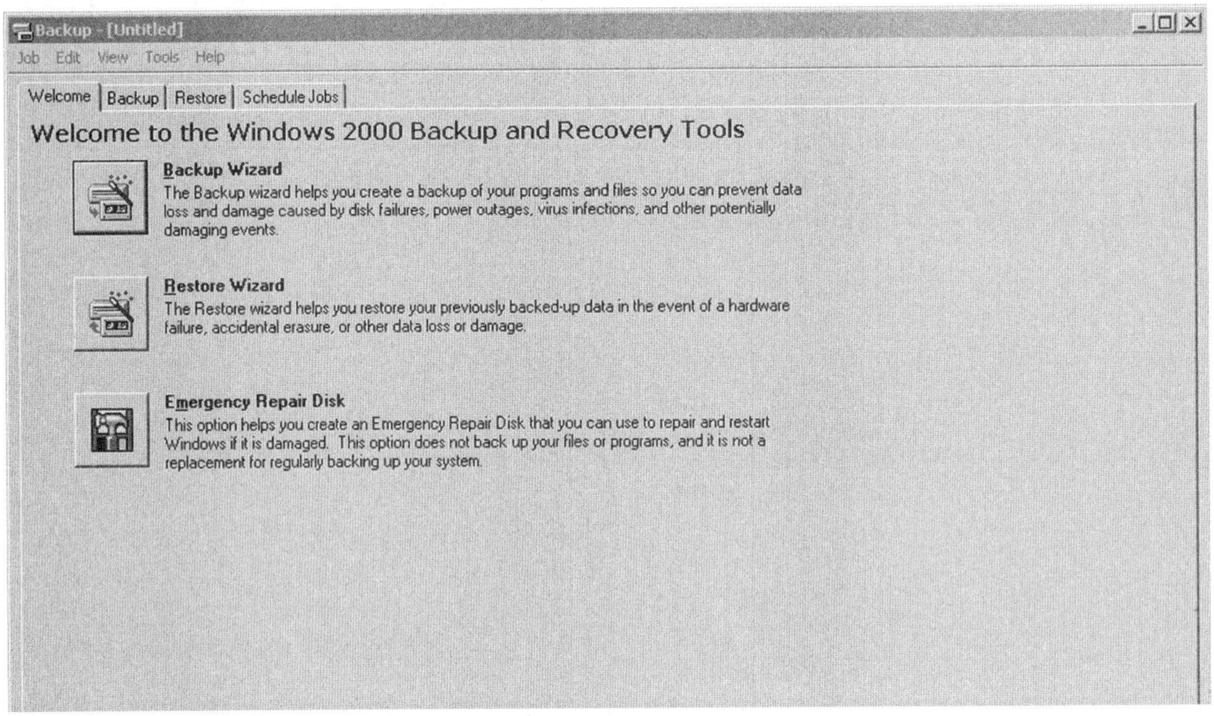

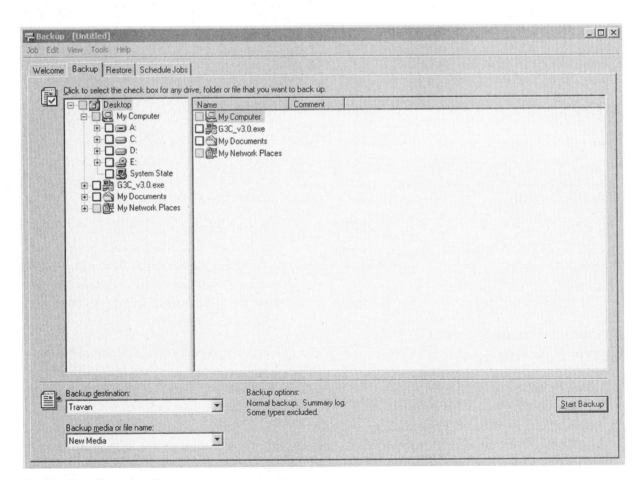

Figure 15.1 The Windows 2000 Backup utility

Figure 15.2 Backup options

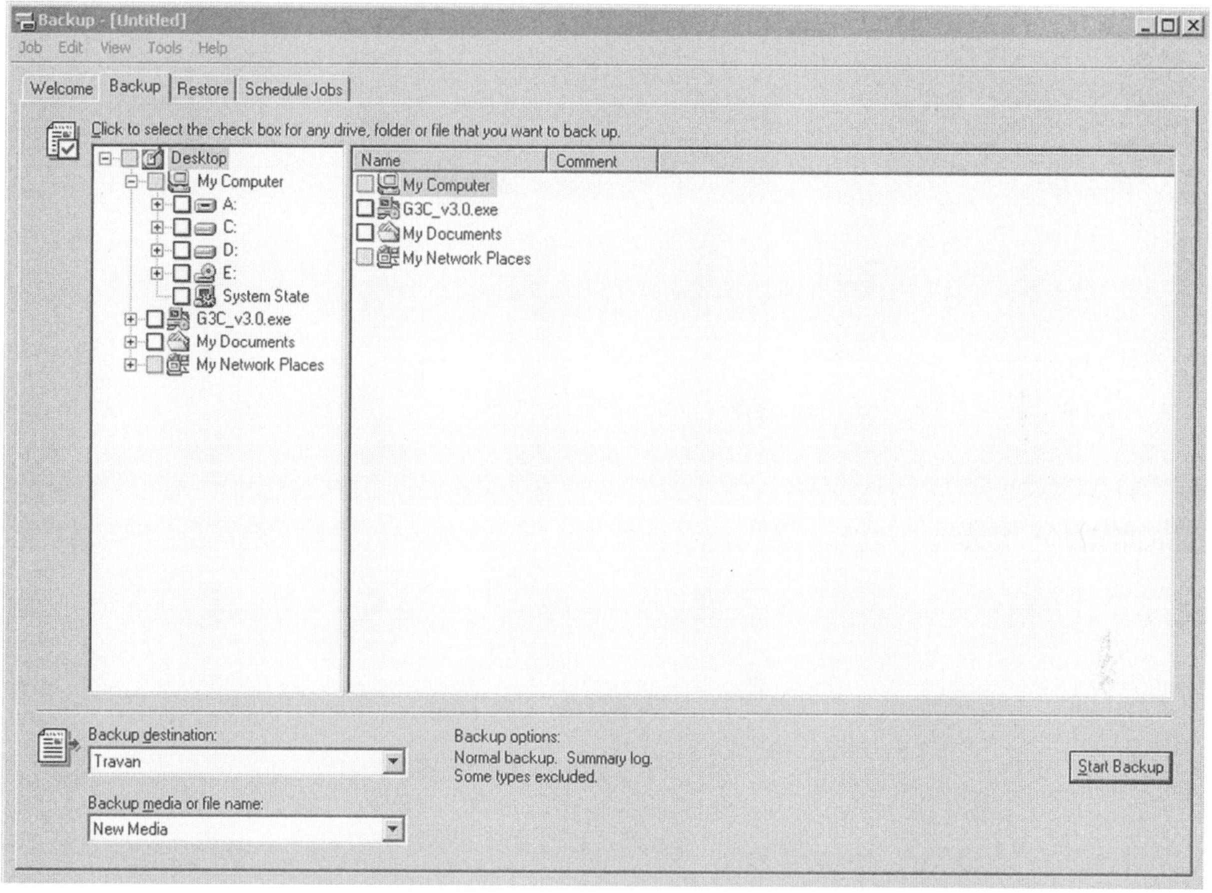

Figure 15.3 Selecting the destination for your backup

selectively choose which files and folders to back up.

4. At the bottom of the screen you have two other options. Backup destination allows you to select where the file is going to be stored. If you have no tape drive installed on your machine, the only option will be File. You will see no scroll bar as appears in the figure. Note in **Figure 15.3** that I have the option to backing up to a miniQIC, Travan, or File. Backup media or file name enables you to indicate the form of medium you are going to use or to select a file name (with full director path) for your backup.

5. Now click the Tools menu and select Options to open a dialog box (**Figure 15.4**). Under Backup Type, you can select Normal, Copy, Differential, Incremental, or

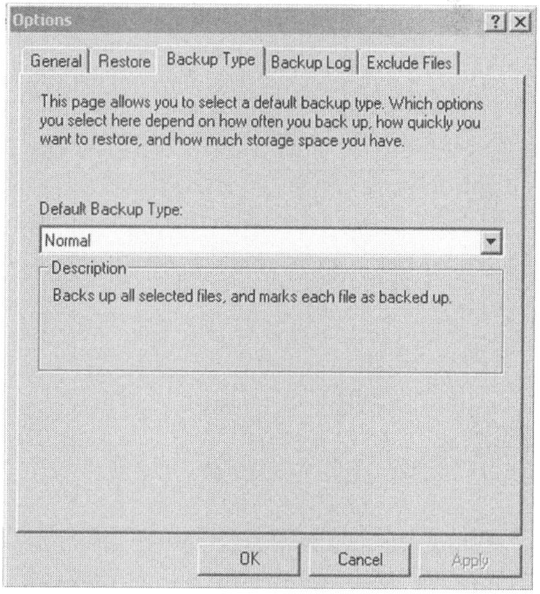

Figure 15.4 Selecting the backup type

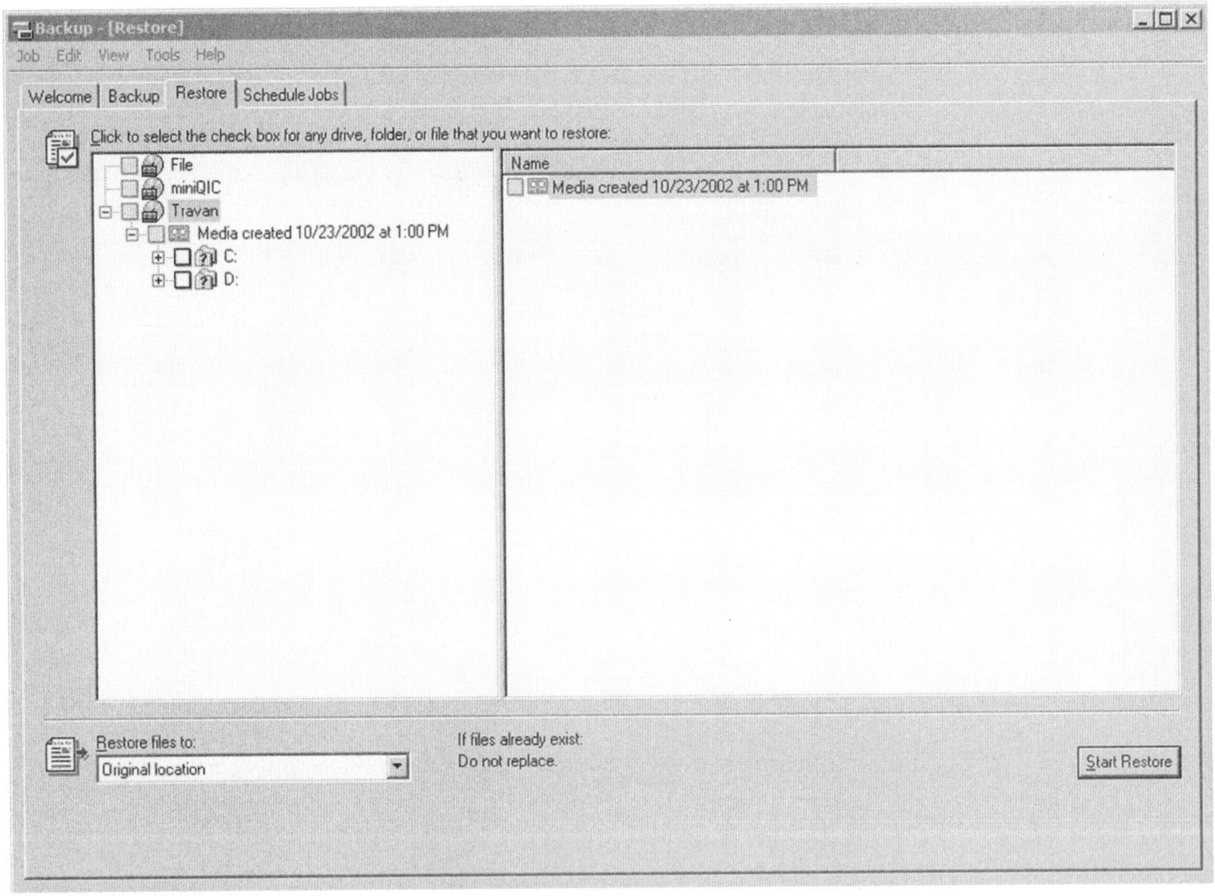

Figure 15.5   Restore options in the Windows 2000 Backup utility

Daily. You will be looking at this section in closer detail in Exercise 2, so for now just click Cancel to close this window.

6. Now you are back at the main Backup window. Click the Restore tab, and you should see a screen like the one in **Figure 15.5**. You are presented with all possible locations on your computer where a backup could exist. If you have no tape drive installed on your machine, the only option available to you will be File.

7. In Figure 15.5, I've opened the Travan option to show that my last backup included my C: drive and my D: drive. In **Figure 15.6**, I've opened the contents of the D: drive. When I did this, my tape drive went into action as it tried to load the contents of that folder. Once it had done that, it rewound the tape. This can take

several minutes on Travan drives. DAT or DLT drives are usually somewhat quicker.

8. Notice that by selecting just a single subdirectory or file (as I've done in Figure 15.6), I can restore just that file or directory. By selecting an entire drive, I will restore the contents of that entire drive.

Exercise 1 Discussion

1. Where do you find the Backup utility in Windows 2000?

2. What is the difference between a differential backup and an incremental backup?

3. What is the difference between copying your files and backing them up?

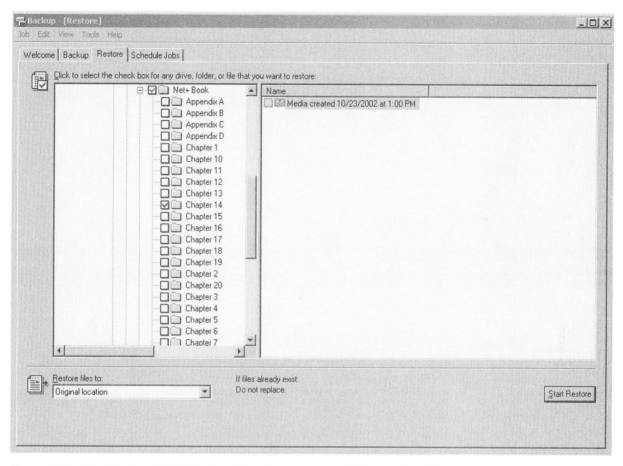

Figure 15.6 The Windows 2000 Backup utility allows you to selectively restore files.

EXERCISE 2: PERFORMING A BACKUP

In this exercise, you will back up a single directory on your hard drive to a file. In order to expedite the procedure, you will select a small directory. Use the one you created using your own first name.

1. On the Backup screen, click the Backup tab. Highlight the hard disk drive that contains your folder, and then click the checkbox next to that folder (**Figure 15.7**).

2. Under Backup destination, select File, and under Backup media or file name, change A:\backup.bkf to C:\backup.bkf. (Note that in the real world, backing up

files from your hard drive to your hard drive is not a very sane practice. If your hard drive fails, the whole thing fails, not just selected directories!)

NOTE: Most backup software still offers the option of backing up your files to floppy. This is a viable option for backing up just a few files, or it can be used when you have a file that is too large to fit onto a floppy disk. The Backup utility will split large files onto several floppy diskettes. If you wish, you can back up your entire hard drive to a collection of floppy diskettes. However, I would like to go on record as saying that the idea of backing up my 40GB hard disk to 27,778 diskettes is not a project that is close to my heart.

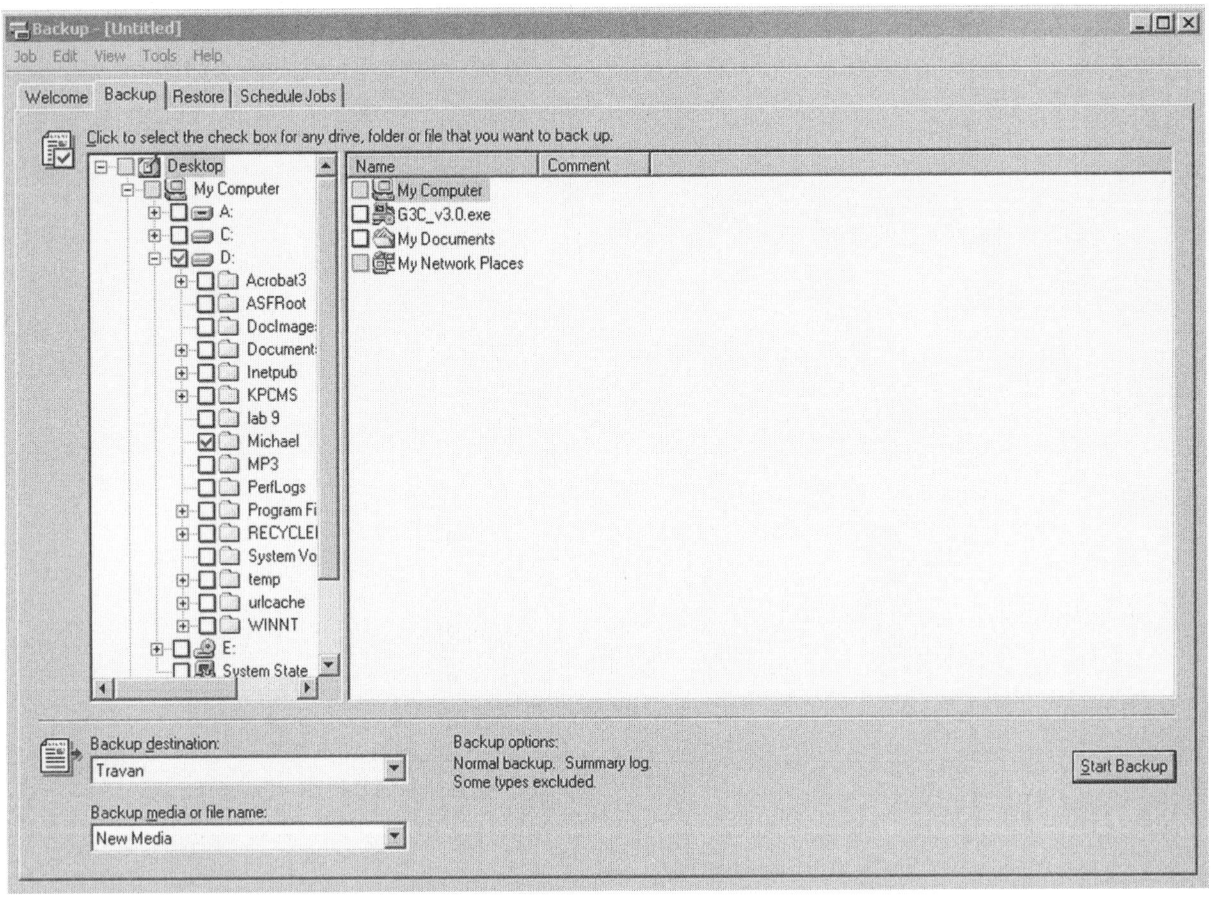

Figure 15.7 Selecting the files to be backed up

3. Click Start Backup. Since you've selected an extremely small backup set, this should only take a second or two. When it is finished you will get a screen like the one in **Figure 15.8**.

4. Here you are informed of the time and date of the backup along with whether it was successful or not. In addition, you can see how long the backup took, how many files were processed, and the total number of bytes that were backed up. Now click the Report button.

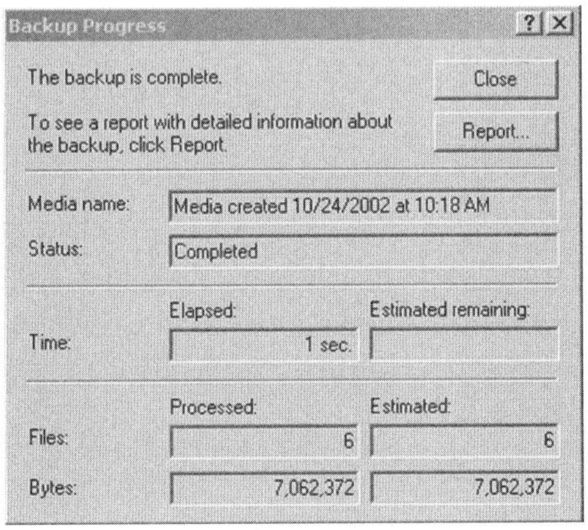

5. For **Figure 15.9**, I performed a backup to my tape drive of the My Documents folder on my hard drive. In order to generate some failure messages, I left Microsoft Word open, along with some documents. Notice the number of files

Figure 15.8 The Backup progress screen

that were skipped because they were in use. This is a key reason why network backups should be performed at a time when the fewest users (none at all, if possible) will be active on the network.

```
backup01.log - Notepad                                                    _ □ X
File  Edit  Format  Help
Backup Status
Operation: Backup
Active backup destination: Travan
Media name: "Media created 10/23/2002 at 1:00 PM"

Backup of "C: "
Backup set #1 on media #1
Backup description: "Set created 10/23/2002 at 1:00 PM"
Backup Type: Normal

Backup started on 10/23/2002 at 1:04 PM.
Backup completed on 10/23/2002 at 1:32 PM.
Directories: 4
Files: 180
Bytes: 826,099,901
Time:   28 minutes and  3 seconds
Media name: "Media created 10/23/2002 at 1:00 PM"

Backup of "D: "
Backup set #2 on media #1
Backup description: "Set created 10/23/2002 at 1:00 PM"
Backup Type: Normal

Backup started on 10/23/2002 at 1:32 PM.
Warning: The file \Documents and Settings\Administrator\Application
Data\Microsoft\Outlook\outcmd.dat in use - skipped.
Warning: The file \Documents and Settings\Administrator\Application
Data\Microsoft\Templates\Normal.dot in use - skipped.
Warning: The file \Documents and Settings\Administrator\Application
Data\Microsoft\Word\AutoRecovery save of Assault on Christian Island, ver 3.asd in
use - skipped.
Warning: The file \Documents and Settings\Administrator\Application
Data\Microsoft\Word\STARTUP\PDFMaker.dot in use - skipped.
Warning: The file \Documents and Settings\Administrator\Local Settings\Application
Data\Microsoft\Outlook\outlook.pst in use - skipped.
```

Figure 15.9   Viewing the Backup log

EXERCISE 2 DISCUSSION

1. What types of destination locations are supported by Windows 2000?

2. Why wouldn't you want to back up your hard drive to floppy diskettes?

3. How can you find out if all of your files were backed up when the operation is completed?

4. If not all the files were backed up, what are some possible causes?

EXERCISE 3: PERFORMING A RESTORE OPERATION

Restoring data to a hard disk drive need not be cause for panic. From your restore file, you have the option of performing a complete restore (as would be required after a hard disk failure once the disk was replaced) or restoring selected files (as might be necessary if a single file is inadvertently deleted, overwritten, or corrupted.) In this exercise, you will delete the folder that you just backed up and use your backup file to recover the lost data.

1. First of all, go into Windows Explorer and delete your folder. Since you shared this folder out in an earlier lab, you will be warned that others might be using the folder. Click OK.

2. In the Backup utility, click the Restore tab. Click the + next to File and then click the + next to the media set you created in Exercise 2 (**Figure 15.10**).

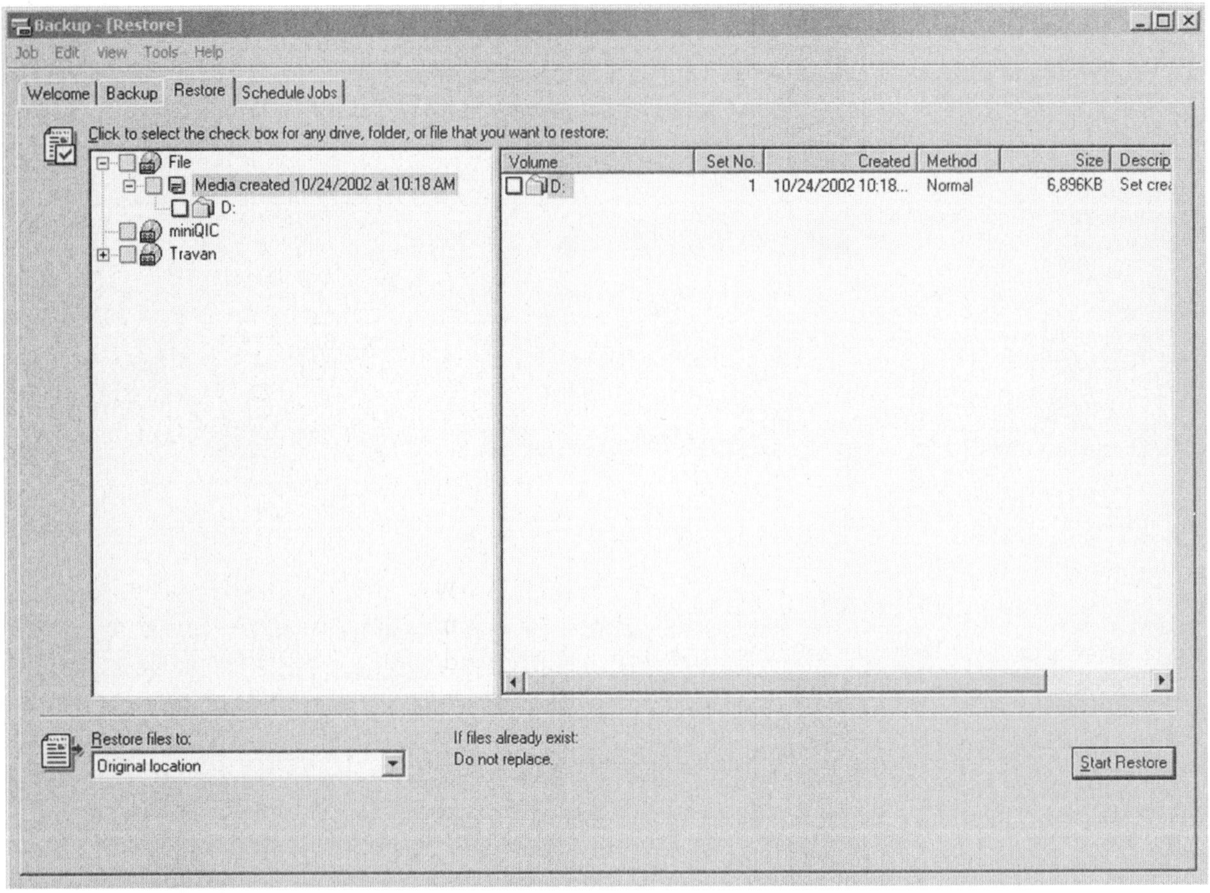

Figure 15.10   Selecting the files to be restored

3. Check the box next to your folder in the left-hand pane. Make sure that the option Restore files to has Original location selected and click the Start Restore button. The Confirm Restore screen will appear (**Figure 15.11**) and offers the choice of starting your Restore or selecting Advanced Options.

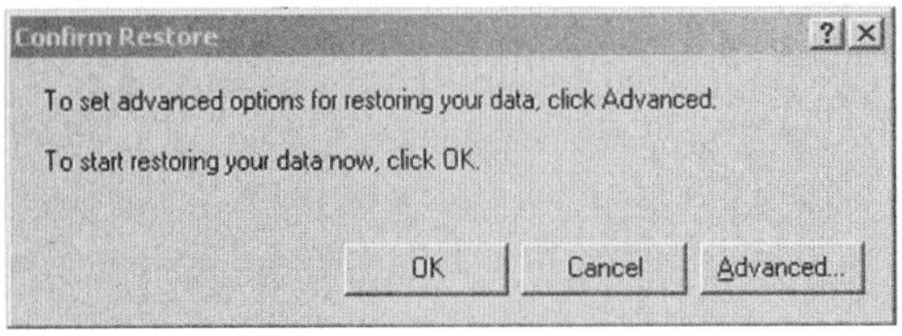

Figure 15.11   The Confirm Restore screen

4. Click the Advanced button. You don't really need to use any of these options, but now is a good time to explore them, since you're here anyway. These options include:

    *   Restore security — This should be checked by default. It makes sure that all permissions assigned to this folder and the files it contains remain intact.

    *   Restore Removable Storage database — Removable Storage is a Windows 2000 service that allows applications to access and share resources stored on removable media. Unless you've installed and configured Removable Storage on your system it is not necessary to select this option.

- Restore junction points, and restore file and folder data under junction points to the original location — A junction point is a physical location on your hard drive that points to another physical location or another storage device. It's a good idea to always leave this box checked. There may be no junction points required, but it's better to have it and not need it than to need it and not have it.

- When restoring replicated data sets, mark the restored data as the primary data for all replicas — This is most likely grayed out on your screen. It assures that information used by the File Replication service knows whether or not this data should be replicated to other servers on the network.

- Preserve existing volume mount points — This particular option really only makes a difference when restoring an entire drive. If you are installing a new drive and it has been partitioned, it is best if this option were not checked. Otherwise new partitions will be created on the drive.

5. For the purposes of this exercise, none of these options is needed. So click Cancel to get back to the Confirm Restore screen and click OK. You'll be prompted to enter the location of the backup file. C:\backup.bkf should be the default location (**Figure 15.12**). Click OK.

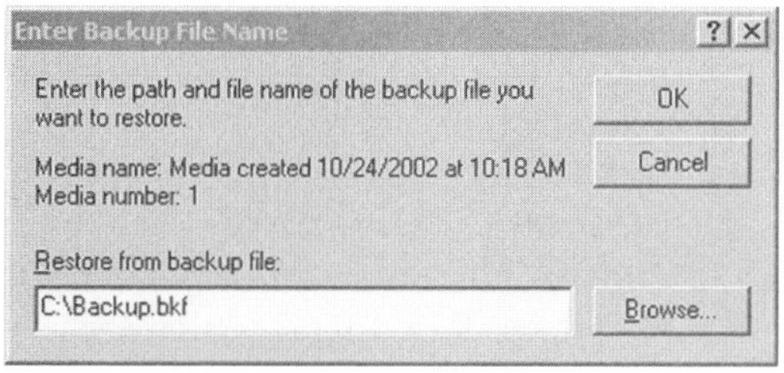

Figure 15.12 Confirming the location of backup files

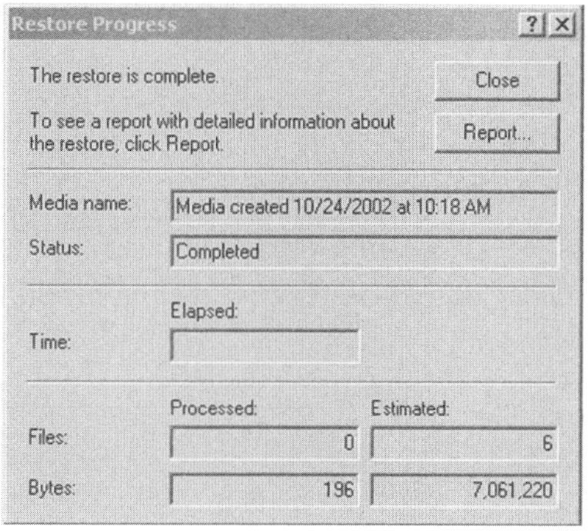

Figure 15.13 The Restore Progress screen

6. You will briefly see a Restore Progress screen flashing the files as they are restored, and then settle into the screen shown in **Figure 15.13**. As you can see, it is identical to the Backup Progress screen you saw in the previous exercise. It, too, offers the option of viewing a report, which will also be identical to the one you looked at in that exercise.

7. Go to Windows Explorer once again. You should be able to browse to your folder and see that all its contents are intact.

EXERCISE 3 DISCUSSION

1. One of your users has inadvertently overwritten a critical file on the server. Can you get just that file back, or do you have to restore the whole system?

2. Name some of the advanced options available in the Backup utility.

EXERCISE 4: SCHEDULING UNATTENDED BACKUPS

In this area, the Windows 2000 Backup utility is a substantial improvement over previous

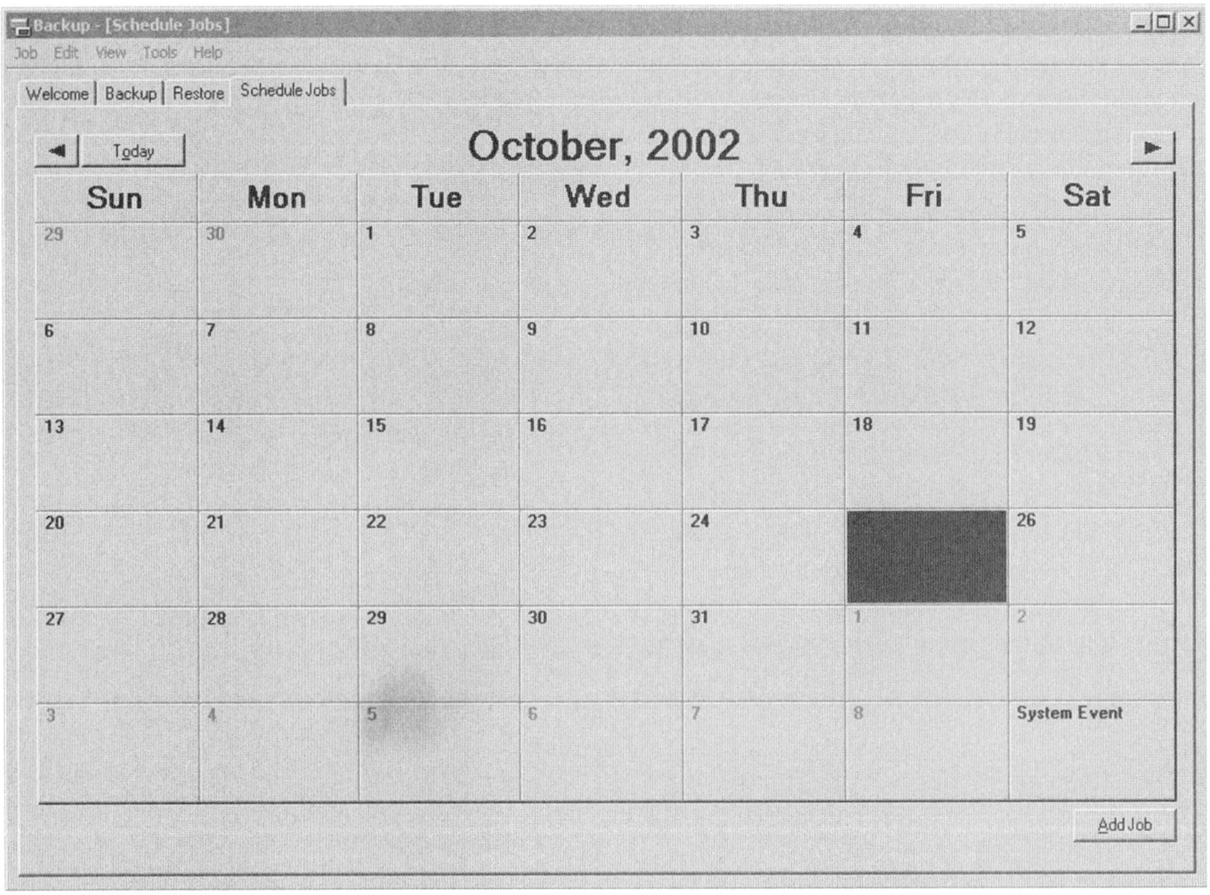

Figure 15.14 The Windows 2000 Backup utility allows you to schedule unattended backups.

versions of Microsoft's Backup utilities. In this exercise, you will see how you can schedule different backups to occur on different days of the week. You'll set up your machines to do a full backup on Friday evening at 8:00 PM and then do incremental backups at the same time Monday through Thursday.

1. In the Backup utility, click the Schedule Jobs tab. This will bring up the screen shown in **Figure 15.14**.

2. Click Add Job in the lower right-hand corner of the screen. This starts the Backup Wizard (**Figure 15.15**).

3. Click Next. The following screen offers three options.

- Back up everything on my computer — Does just what it suggests. However, don't put too much faith in what it says. As you saw earlier, open or locked files will not be backed up.

- Back up selected files, drives, or network data — Allows you to pick and choose what material should be backed up.

- Only back up the System State data — This information includes the

Figure 15.15   Adding a new job to the backup schedule

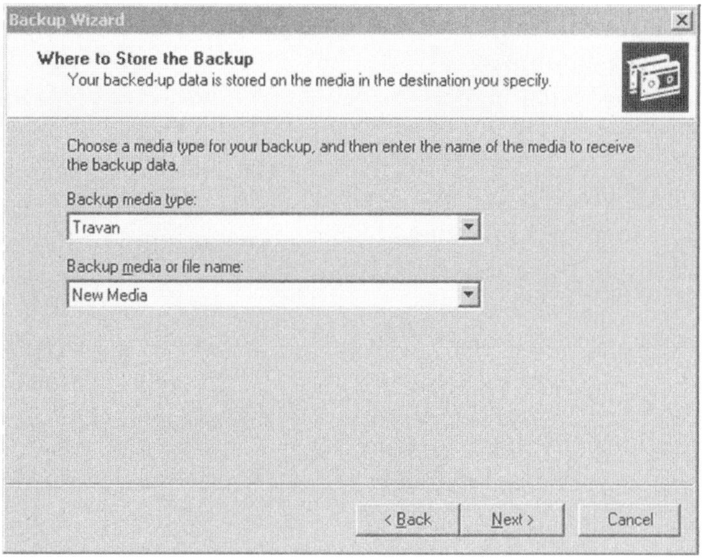

Figure 15.16   Selecting the destination device for your scheduled backups

files that make up the registry, the COM+ registration database, and all system boot files.

4. Select Back up everything on my computer and click Next. This brings up the screen in **Figure 15.16**, where you are prompted to select the destination for your backup. In my illustration, I selected my Travan drive. You should select a file name under Backup media or file name. Put the backup in the directory you created under your own name, and call it Backup.

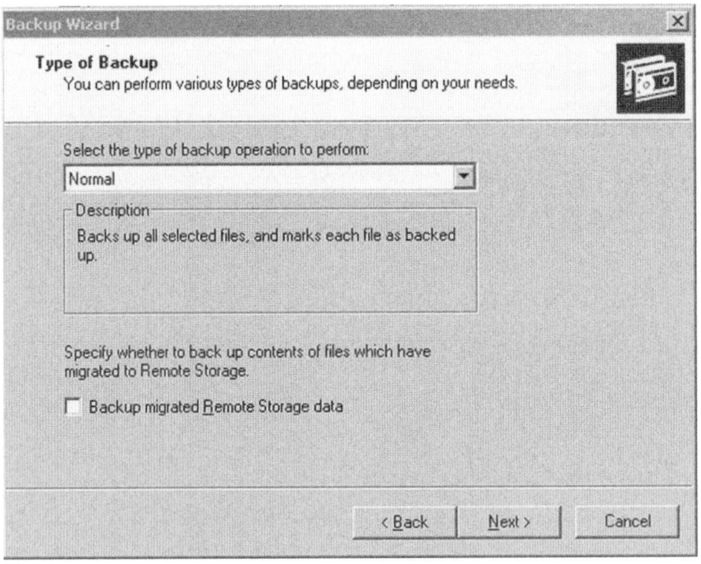

Figure 15.17 Selecting the type of backup to be performed

5. In **Figure 15.17**, you're prompted to enter the type of backup you'll be performing. The options are:

   • Normal — Copies all selected files and clears the attribute bits, marking the files as backed up. If an entire drive was selected, this is the equivalent of a Full backup.

   • Copy — It copies all selected files but does *not* clear the attribute bits. Therefore, the files will not be marked as backed up.

   • Incremental — Copies any files that were added or changed since the last Normal or Incremental backup. It clears the attribute bits, marking the files as backed up. All subsequent Incremental backups will now back up all files changed since the last Incremental backup.

   • Differential — This selection copies all files that were added or changed since the last Normal or Incremental backup, but does *not* clear the attribute bits. Therefore files will not be marked as backed up. All subsequent differential backups will back up all files added or changed since the last Normal or Incremental backup, and not just those that changed since the last Differential backup.

   • Daily — Copies only files that were added or changed on the day the backup is created. The attribute bit is not cleared.

6. Since you are creating a full backup, select Normal, and click Next. The Backup Wizard now asks you how you want to back your data up (**Figure 15.18**). Two independent options are offered.

   • Verify data after backup — This option compares each copy of the file to the original when the backup has been completed. This can add a substantial amount of time to the backup but adds security for your data.

   • Use hardware compression, if available — This allows you to pack more

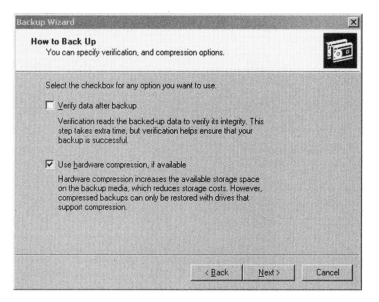

Figure 15.18 Configuring how the backup is to be done

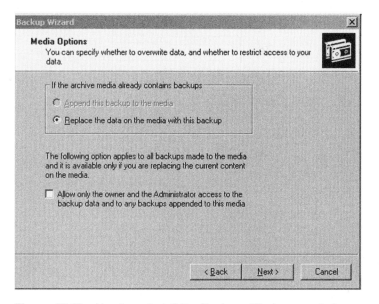

Figure 15.19 You have to tell the Backup utility how media is to be handled.

data onto a single tape and reduces the amount of time it takes for a backup to be completed.

Just leave the default options selected here, and click Next.

7. Next you'll see the Media Options screen (**Figure 15.19**). Normally, you would be using the same tapes over and over again. In that case, you would make sure that the option Replace the data on the media with this backup is selected. If the data is sensitive data, you can add a bit more security by selecting the option Allow only the owner and the Administrator access to the data and to any backup appended to this media. The latter option is not selected by default. Accept the default settings and click Next.

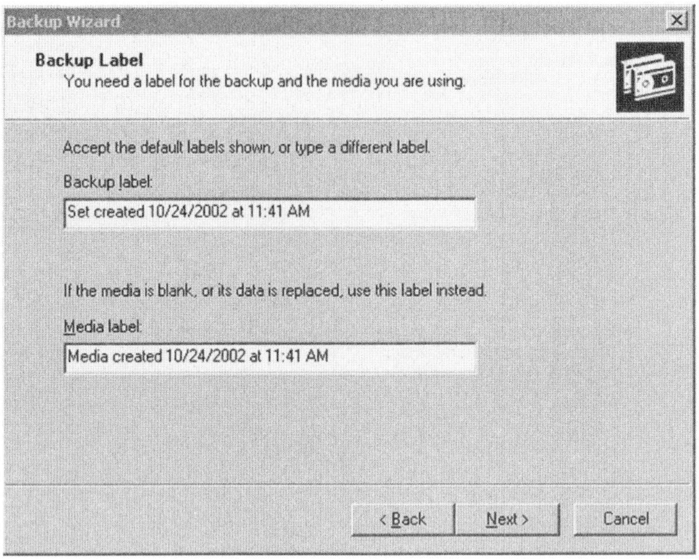

Figure 15.20 The Windows 2000 Backup utility is even gracious enough to remind you to label your backup tapes.

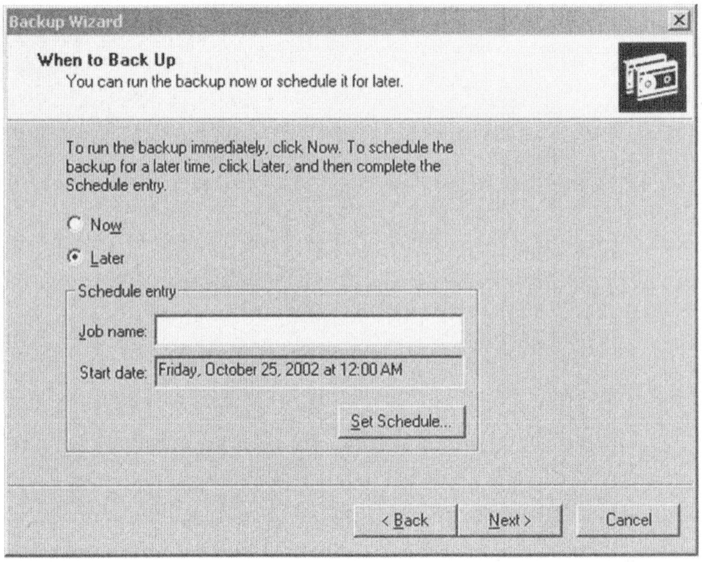

Figure 15.21 You must tell the scheduler what time you want these backups to occur. Choose a time when there will be the fewest users on the network.

8. The Backup Label screen now appears (**Figure 15.20**). This is the information that you should write onto the label of the tape before storing it. Click Next.

9. Now you'll be prompted about when you want your backup to occur (**Figure**

15.21). Select Later and give your job a name. Call it Weekly Full.

10. Now click the Set Schedule button. Under Schedule Task, select Weekly. Under Start Time, select 12:00 AM. Under Schedule Task Weekly select 1 for

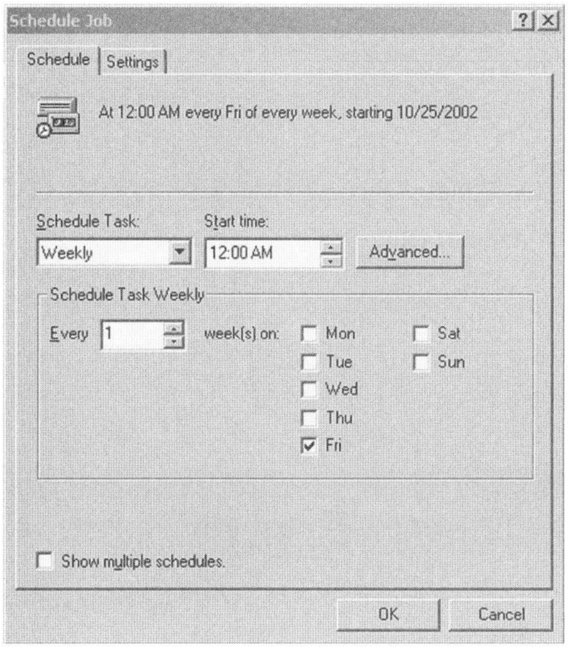

Figure 15.22 Scheduling daily or weekly events

Completing the Backup Wizard screen as shown in **Figure 15.23**. Click Finish and you're done.

12. Now, on the Schedule Jobs calendar, little icons with a blue N (for Normal) will appear on all Fridays from this date forward.

13. To schedule daily differential backups to occur, repeat the above procedure except for two key differences:

    In step 5, where you configured backup type, select Differential.

    In step 9, under Job name call it Daily Differential. In step 10, where the events are scheduled, select Weekly as before, but check the boxes for Mon, Tue, Wed, and Thu.

    Finish the Wizard and now icons will appear on all Mondays through Thursdays with a green D (for Differential). Your calendar should now resemble **Figure 15.24**.

Every and click the Friday checkbox, as in **Figure 15.22**. Make sure that all other days are deselected.

11. Click OK and on the Backup Wizard screen, click Next. This will bring up the

14. Now the most important step of all. Make sure there is a tape in the drive for

Figure 15.23 Finishing the Backup Wizard

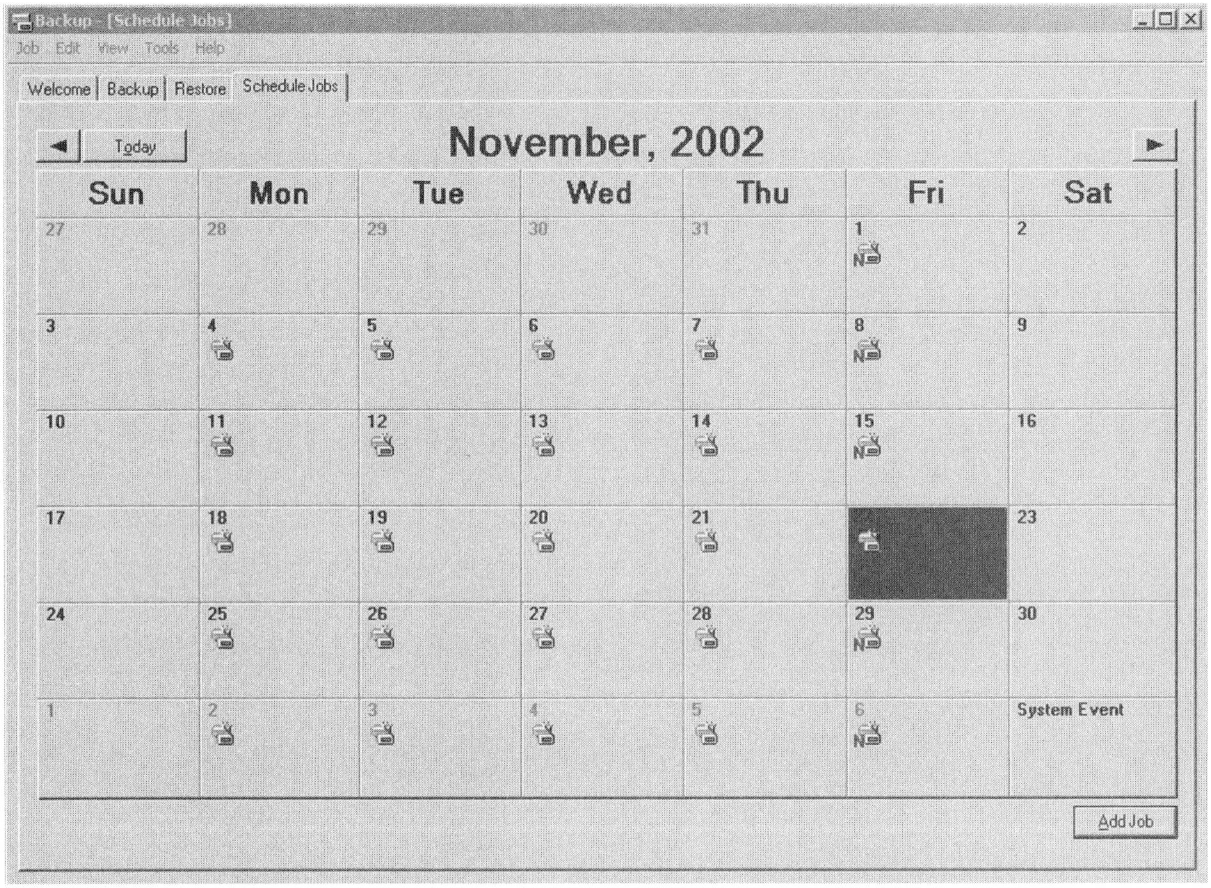

Figure 15.24 A Scheduling Calendar with events in place

each day an event is scheduled. It may seem like a no-brainer, but an empty tape drive is undoubtedly the most common cause of backup failure there is.

NOTE: You may notice if you look carefully that there is no option in the Backup Scheduler to delete a scheduled event. If you need to delete a scheduled backup for any reason, open Control Panel and double-click Scheduled Tasks. Highlight the job you want to blow away and press the delete key on your keyboard. The program will ask you if you're sure. Click OK and the jobs are gone.

EXERCISE 4 DISCUSSION

1. You want to schedule your server to perform a Full backup every week, starting at 12:00 AM on Saturday. But you want your daily backups to be Differential backups and to run at 10:00 PM every other night. How do you keep these from conflicting?

2. What is the primary cause of backup failure in unattended scheduled backups?

3. You need to delete one or more scheduled backup jobs, but there is no delete function in the Backup utility. How do you do that?